RUDI

In His Own Words

Rudra Press
P.O. Box 1973
Cambridge, Massachusetts 02238

Compiled and edited by Jennifer Cross
Cover design by Milton Glaser
Book design by Caroline Kutil
Photos by Barry Kaplan

Manufactured in the United States of America.

Library of Congress Cataloging-in-Publication Data

Rudrananda, Swami, 1928-1973.
   Rudi: in his own words / Swami Rudrananda (Rudi); introduc-
tion by Swami Chetanananda.
      p.   cm.
   Includes index.
   ISBN 0-915801-20-5
   1. Spiritual life.
BL624.R794 1990   90-20083
291.4 – dc20   CIP

RUDI

In His Own Words

Swami Rudrananda (Rudi)

Introduction by Swami Chetanananda

Rudra Press
Cambridge, Massachusetts

I am not here to give you answers. I am here to give you the energy so that you can get your own answers and find within you that which you are.

— RUDI

Contents

RUDI

In His Own Words

Introduction

by Swami Chetanananda

A spiritual teacher exists to challenge and disturb the boundaries of our identity. That is his or her real purpose. The point of disturbing the balance and structure of our identity is to cause us to look more deeply within ourselves and to examine the nature of our own source. Over time, we begin to recognize the universal, infinite nature of our individualized consciousness.

Swami Rudrananda — or Rudi, as he was known — was my teacher. He was a student first of the Shankaracharya of Puri and then of Bhagawan Nityananda, a great saint of South India. When Rudi met Nityananda, the tremendous power of the saint's presence changed Rudi's entire life. While Rudi had always pursued spiritual growth, he became even more deeply dedicated to his spiritual work and returned to the states to teach a small group of students of his own in New York.

After Nityananda passed away in 1961, Rudi traveled regularly to Ganeshpuri to visit Nityananda's

shrine and to study with Swami Muktananda. In
1966, Swami Muktananda initiated Rudi as a swami,
naming him "Rudrananda," which means "the bliss of
Rudra." Rudra is a fiery aspect of the Hindu god
Shiva. The significance of the event was that the old
Rudi, born Albert Rudolph in Brooklyn, New York,
was now dead to the world. Rudi continued to teach
in the United States, and over time started some ten
ashrams across the country and in Europe. At the
same time, he maintained a business, providing work
for his mother and younger brother.

When I met Rudi in 1971, he had been teaching in New York City for some years. I had gone to
New York to meet him at the suggestion of an ac-
quaintance. When I walked into his store, I took one
look at him and my heart broke. I am not ordinarily
an emotional person, but my knees turned to jelly
and I started to cry. It took me no more than five sec-
onds to recognize that his presence in my own life
was the most important thing that would ever happen to me. Indeed, in Rudi, I found the fulfillment of
my life.

Rudi often described the relationship, or the
flow, between the teacher and the student as spiritual
nourishment. This flow is a giving on the part of the
teacher who, in turn, takes on the tensions and restric-
tions of the student in order to digest and dissolve
them. Furthermore, the teacher is committed to
standing in harmony with the student until this process of transmitting the energy has matured and the
student is fully established in the recognition of his or
her own highest consciousness.

This installation might take thirty-six years to complete, depending upon the intensity of the contact and the discipline and determination of the student. It could also take less than three. This depends more on the student than on the teacher. Rudi described the process as nourishment because he wanted to engender in his students a sense of responsibility. We ourselves had to reach for the teaching. We had to internalize, absorb, and digest it. It was up to us to make it a part of our own system. When we can do this, then the nourishment itself renews our vitality and energy. It washes away tensions and brings about within us a sense of fulfillment and well-being.

The contact between student and teacher is not something that we can understand from an intellectual point of view. Every student is different, every teacher is different, and the creative contact between the two is always a unique and extraordinary moment — a universe within itself. This universe is the main thing that the teacher wants the student to examine. To recognize what this contact really is, and to live from that recognition — this is the highest realization.

It is the recognition that the power of Life Itself, the consciousness of the teacher, and our own individual consciousness are all one. From that moment of realization onward, we turn our attention not outward toward any other person, but inside ourselves. We remain focused on that infinite moment of contact between our mind, our heart, and our highest Self. That moment of contact encompasses every individual that we encounter. Regardless of the specific relationship we may have with them, we encounter an inherent balance and equality.

This equality exists in the student-teacher relationship as well. The respect that the student demonstrates toward the teacher is the respect one extends to someone who has given their life to mastering an understanding and to sharing it with others. With respect of this kind, there is no issue of dominant-subordinate or superior-inferior. We continue to cultivate the relationship while, at the same time, we recognize the infinite moment of contact to be nothing but pure, universal consciousness. We are That, the teacher is That, and there is no differentiation or break between the two. This is what we experienced in Rudi.

Rudi lived a simple life. Each day he got up and prepared breakfast for the few students who lived with him in his brownstone in Manhattan's East Village. Then he went to work at his oriental art store just around the corner. He always wore the same thing — a plain orange T-shirt, khaki pants, and sandals. In the winter, he wore socks.

Rudi was a deeply quiet being whose attention was turned within, and who was dedicated to sharing his own inner work with whoever approached him. People came into his store from many different places and for many different reasons. Rabbis, Catholic priests and nuns, Buddhist and Hindu monks, art dealers from Thailand and Japan, museum curators, famous actors and politicians, browsing customers, and disturbed street people all entered his store at one point or another. Rudi was the same with every one of them. He handled each person with grace, charm, dignity, humor, and a loving simplicity that was both touching and powerful.

He left his store at six o'clock every evening and returned home to lead a kundalini yoga class. The class, to which he refers in this book, was an exchange that promoted our ability to experience the inner state in which he himself was immersed. Afterwards he would talk for a while about some aspect of our spiritual work. By ten or ten-thirty, Rudi and those of us who lived in his house would go to bed.

Rudi came from humble surroundings. He had a difficult upbringing and, unlike his counterparts in India, did not have easy access to a great spiritual culture. He was a man who, through his own dedication and great faith in God, overcame every obstacle and limitation in his path and grew to become a spiritual giant.

Despite having been initiated into the role, Rudi was not a swami in the traditional sense of the word. He was a monk, in that he lived a deeply simple life. At the same time, he was not a monk, insofar as he supported himself and lived among his family. He defied stereotypes. He felt that part of our spiritual work involves the full acceptance of who and what we are. His own life demonstrated the freedom that we all have to be ourselves while working to attain our liberation.

Furthermore, Rudi had strong opinions about what was spiritual and what was not. He did not approve of much of what often goes on under the name of spirituality. He talked, instead, about growing — about the flow of energy within us and the release of tensions. He talked about transcending ourselves

and about how this process entails an endless amount
of work.

He challenged the tendency to engage in one
form or another of spiritual materialism through the
pursuit of phenomena such as astral travel, past lives,
visions, or miracles. This, he said, is nothing more
than the need for external validation of our inner
work. If we can levitate for ten minutes, we think we
are closer to God. This is a false sign of growth. Rudi
taught us instead to focus on our inner work. The
work itself and the transformation that it brings about
— these are the real miracles.

Rudi gave us an exercise intended to purify
our bodies, remove the blocks and tensions we
brought with us, and enable us to feel the flow of
energy within us. This was an exercise involving control of the breath. This practice has a depth to it that
is not immediately apparent. For a beginning student,
it involves control of the physical breath. At another
level, we are cultivating our awareness of the pulsation of energy within us. We tune into and are simply
aware of the fluctuation of the various levels of this
pulsation. Thus, it is a practice with many dimensions. But at the beginning level, it is a means by
which we learn to release tensions and allow the creative energy within us to flow.

In teaching us, Rudi was a hard-nosed trainer
and one who was demanding of his students. He insisted that we rise above our own level of work to participate at his, so that we could maintain an on-going,
living relationship with him. He would do as much
as he could for whoever came to him but, fundamen-
tally, he did not want to be attached to people or to

have anyone become attached to him. He was not interested in having a following or in setting up a personality cult. He never allowed any of us to get tangled up in him. He wanted to be free himself and did not want people to become bound to him. So, as we developed, he pushed us away from him and forced us to become stronger still.

Rudi believed in discipline. He was dedicated to his own inner work and he did not appreciate anything but dedication in others. He was not tolerant of dilettantism among his students, just as he was not tolerant of laziness or of the confusion that comes from an unwillingness to do one's own work. For him the process of growing spiritually was a simple thing: either you were doing it or you were not. There was no need for confusion about that.

He felt that once we make the fundamental decision to undertake spiritual work and devote ourselves to it, then it is either happening or it is not. There are no complex emotional questions to be dealt with, no dilemmas or dichotomies to untwine. People are either working inside to allow the tensions of their lives to unravel, or they are struggling in what he would call stupidity and tension. He had no value for that kind of complexity. Indeed, he used to say that life is profound only in its simplicity.

He was serious about only one thing, and he was intensely serious about that. He devoted himself to sharing with people the experience of the specialness that exists deeply within the heart and soul. He was interested in transmitting to people the tools and the skills by which they could come to understand this specialness, cultivate and live from it, and eventually allow it to permeate the entire field of their everyday experience.

Furthermore, Rudi was not idealistic. He was profoundly pragmatic, and was interested only in what works. The idea of "work" permeates everything he said and did. But with this emphasis, he was also exercising a subtle understanding. If our inner energy is a seed, it is true that we do need to cultivate it. Nevertheless, it is the seed itself that unfolds and flowers. We may plant and water it, we may make sure it has sunlight, but then *it* does the actual work. Our ability to focus our attention on growing and then get out of our own way is what Rudi meant by surrender.

A tribute to the vitality of Rudi's work was the fact that he left us with a living tradition. At the same time, Rudi was particular that the people who carried on this tradition have his direct blessing or, in his absence, the permission of one of his chosen successors. Although there are several people around the country who claim to have Rudi's permission to teach, the only ones still teaching who had his blessing to do so are myself, and Stewart Perin in New York. I am therefore sometimes appalled at the number of people who met Rudi once or twice and yet claim to have received his permission to teach.

Anybody can go out and declare him- or herself a disciple of one teacher or another. This does not mean that the teacher has, in fact, taken on the person as a student. Nor does it mean that such a person has achieved the spiritual maturity or the stability in the highest state of unfoldment necessary to lead another person into a similar degree of awareness.

The blessing of the teacher is some guarantee that he or she both recognizes and vouches for this maturity and stability. This was something about which Rudi felt strongly.

In the development of Eastern spirituality in the United States, Rudi was probably the first person to point out that it is the substance of Eastern spiritual teaching that interests us, not the form. At a time when many people were denying their own social and cultural backgrounds and reaching out to encompass another culture, whether Indian, Tibetan, Buddhist, drug, or hip, Rudi emphatically insisted that people could only grow in their own cultural soil. It is not possible to transplant a person from one soil to another and expect them to grow. Furthermore, he insisted that a person was not in this world to *realize* any kind of culture, but rather to transcend *all* culture and society.

At the same time, Rudi felt that the rejectionism prevalent in many religious traditions is useless. He also felt that it is not necessary to retreat to the rarefied atmosphere of a monastery. Instead, growing requires that we be exposed to life — to a diversity, breadth, and depth of experience. This is what allows us to encompass the different aspects of life and to take them in as nourishment. In this way, we begin to understand the underlying simplicity and power of Life Itself. We transcend prejudice, intolerance, and judgmentalism; we arrive at the universal state that is the objective of every spiritual practice.

When Rudi uses the term "detachment," he means detachment from everything related to materialism and materiality. We cannot completely detach ourselves from the circumstances of our life, since Life Itself is our very essence. We can, however, transcend the limited understanding through which we see our circumstances. In transcending this materialism, we begin to recognize the essence of our experience, and to go beyond the superficial. This enables us to participate in the finest and highest level of experience itself — that is, our universal nature.

Rudi advocated remaining involved in our responsibilities in the world. Not attached to them, but involved. He felt that it was inappropriate to "tune in and drop out," as so many people were advocating at the time. Rather, he felt that we should tune in and *transcend*, even as we fulfill our responsibilities and remain within our many relationships. Then, through the various exercises of our spiritual work, we should address the tensions that arise in these different contexts. Resolving the tensions, we find a new balance and a deeper flow within our work and our relationships. This, in turn, leads us to a clearer understanding of our own nature and to the nature of experience itself. This theme of rising above tensions appears over and over again in Rudi's work.

Another theme that flows through his teaching is the discussion of death and rebirth as an important part of our spiritual experience. By death and rebirth, however, he means something different from what we often take these terms to mean. Often we see a crisis in our lives, or the appearance of any strong tension at all, as a manifestation of a death and rebirth experience. Then we get caught up in the crisis or the tension, relying upon it as proof that something important is happening in our spiritual life. To do this, however, is to bring to a mundane level the rebirth experience to which Rudi was referring, whereas a true death and rebirth experience is a profound change at a deep inner level.

Most people miss the true death and rebirth experiences in their lives because they don't have a subtle awareness of their inner state. Consequently, these experiences simply go by. Rudi used to say that miracles are happening all the time. Since we are not conscious of them, however, we miss them. Either that, or we panic when we see the changes that they bring about in our lives.

Things naturally fall away as we grow. If we are going to change and be transformed, then aspects of what we were will have to depart or fall away. A tree loses its leaves every year; a plant loses its flowers; no blossom stays attached all year long. Birds shed their feathers; snakes shed their skins. Every creature that goes through some kind of recreative experience faces such changes. So, we manifest the degree to which we are spiritually evolved in our ability to rise above the material symptoms of this spiritual change in order to begin to engage the change itself. We become able to release the people, places, and things in our life.

This is a profound and difficult experience. It involves shedding the past. With it, we therefore also transcend any notion of future. A spiritual death and rebirth experience occurs when we transcend the continuum of time and space to participate in the infinitely present, infinitely powerful, infinitely full and dynamic power of Life Itself. It occurs when we transcend the manifestations of creativity and enter into the pure creative process. This was what Rudi's own life was about.

Rudi said repeatedly that we are not here to think about living; we are here simply to live. We are not here to try to figure out life; we are here to open ourselves to it. We do not grow strong by trying to protect ourselves; we grow strong by exposing ourselves. We do not develop a deep understanding of life by intellectualizing or discussing it; we discover a deep understanding of life by doing quiet inner work in a deep way.

Rudi's own life was a pragmatic demonstration of the value of spiritual practice in the real world and its capacity to benefit not only the individual, but the whole environment. I have met many spiritual teachers in my travels, but never have I met anybody who surpassed Rudi in spiritual attainment. He was immersed in that profoundly simple, utterly powerful joy that exists at the center of the heart of every human being. Moreover, he had the capacity to share that joy with people in the simplest of ways. The simplicity of these acts on his part were what had the most profound impact on the people whose lives he touched.

Rudi loved God. He was willing to sacrifice everything in his physical life for the sake of his commitment to that love. Everything he said and did expressed the depth of this commitment. He lived in the readiness to sacrifice himself in the fire of that love, so that those of us around him who participated in it through him would be able to experience and understand it more fully within ourselves.

For me, the main message of Rudi's life has been that there is an extraordinary opportunity available to each one of us as human beings not only to discover our own divine potential, but also to unfold and express it. Rudi showed me how to find within myself the love that he himself demonstrated every day. His example also showed me how to express it. Furthermore, he demonstrated that such love exists in each and every human being. It is our contact with this love that makes every place we are our home. It makes any person we are with a part of our family, and any food we have to eat, be it simple or elaborate, a great banquet. It makes our life a continuous experience of simple joy and great happiness.

This book is not the story of Rudi's life. Rudi's history has been told many times. Moreover, presenting his life story is deceptive. The pieces of his life do not add up to what he ultimately became. He was a subtle phenomenon that cannot be appreciated from a biographical point of view. Nothing in his personal history justifies the extraordinary spiritual state he attained. His childhood, his upbringing, his schooling — none of these explains what he was. To a great extent, Rudi was a product of his teaching. This book is an attempt to show something of what that teaching was.

CAMBRIDGE, MA
1990

Growing

Spirituality is the only way to deal with life as it is. Everything else is hiding.

Our purpose on this earth is to grow. We are no different than any other living thing; we take in one form of energy and are supposed to give out a higher form of energy. We grow by recycling, by taking in tensions and poison and giving off life, in the same way that a tree, a bush, or any blade of grass on the earth takes in carbon dioxide and gives off oxygen. A human being is meant to live by taking in lesser things, by overcoming situations. This is how we grow. We don't just work for three or four weeks and assume we have evolved to a point where we are superior to other people. Growth takes place every single day. A tree or a bush has to grow every day. If it stops growing, it is dead.

The energy that you consciously drag out of life fuels your growth. During the day, instead of reacting to everything externally, you consciously draw in energy and bring it through all the different energy centers in yourself. This energy rises to the top of your head, and it stays there, creating a reservoir that eventually overflows. Then it secretes into the brain a higher form of nourishment. If you look through any book of oriental sculpture, you will see on the top of the head of each of the statues some kind of a crown, or rise. That rise has to do with this energy. The higher creative energy comes to the top of the head and then nourishes a person.

Kundalini yoga allows you to refine your energy and get stronger energy. Energy is a wealth. If you are living in a dirty rooming house, there are plenty of opportunities for fights. But if you have wealth, you can rise above many situations. You live in a better place in yourself and in a better relationship to the world. You relate to the tensions only when your energy is lower than the tensions. When your energy rises, when it finally becomes something you are consciously in control of, you realize you can't do anything about *this*, but you can do something about *that*. You have control. You are not compulsive in your involvements, you are conscious. This gives you a choice, and having a choice, again, saves energy. You are detached from life to a much greater degree, and because of that you have the benefit of your own energy. Regardless of what you are doing, you are not involved to the point that you lose yourself.

The classical description of kundalini yoga technique is very involved, but the principle of kundalini yoga is basically simple. You use your own energy consciously to free you from the tensions within your own body, mind, and soul and to allow your own energy to rise to a level at which you have communication with other dimensions of energy. It sounds complicated, but it is actually a very simple process wherein you begin to release tensions within yourself. Once those tensions are released, your own energy increases, and this brings about changes within you. Your breathing changes; your muscle structure changes. The life flow within you increases, which allows you to mature and evolve.

Kundalini yoga is used to collect within yourself and bring through your own chemistry the energy that is in the universe. A human being is only able to do that by internalizing energy and bringing it through his or her system. The chakras referred to in Indian mythology and spirituality, such as in the brain and the heart, are energy centers that have within them the capacity to retain the richness of psychic experience. These chakras must be developed so that the energy can be drawn in and consciously brought from chakra to chakra, or from center to center, all the way down through a human being, through his or her sex center and up the spinal column to the top of the head.

Eventually kundalini yoga brings about a complete changeover in the instrumentation of a human being. As we go through this process of taking in energy, we refine ourselves and our mechanism changes. Our heart has to open and expand, the lungs have to open and expand, the eyes have to change, all the muscles and all the senses of the brain have to

go through a transformation. In the Bible this is sym-
bolized by Christ's making a blind man see. But it is
really just a matter of the increased function of any
organ or any muscle that is receiving better nourishment. You, with your own consciousness of pursuing
a higher creative life, can draw this nourishment in
through your own instrument.

The basic principles that are used in kundalini
yoga are your own will, your breathing, and a very
simple form and structure. It is a process of internalizing instead of externalizing experience.

As you grow and as this nourishment expands
in you, your reaction to outside situations can change.
You are no longer limited by the low level of energy
you previously had or by the tensions that formerly
affected your capacity to relate to a situation. As you
open and bring more energy into yourself, you are
freer, more detached, and better able to get above the
situation. You don't react to the ordinary tension that
you reacted to previously. You don't look at people
and take them on the ordinary levels of relationship.
You can make a conscious effort; you can go inside
yourself and detach from, instead of automatically
becoming the victim of, your own tensions. You have
an increased consciousness, which allows you to separate yourself a little from your experience and not
jump into an involvement or a tension.

This separation occurs with people who are
very finely bred. They are well trained, they are
taught control, so they can ordinarily observe a situation with more detachment. Everything we aspire to
spiritually has to bring us, on an ordinary physical

level, this additional quality, this additional breeding, which gives us the ability to be more conscious with people and to practice all the basic rules of good manners, behavior, and positive interaction with human beings.

I will give you a wonderful example. About a year ago, an insane lady came into my store, carrying a shopping bag full of empty Coca-Cola and Pepsi-Cola bottles. She was really crazy. At that time I was deeply in my own growth. I felt as if I was out on the end of a seesaw. I could not afford to react to her, and I was very aware of it. I could not afford to feel anything against her, and I could not find it in myself to tell her to leave, because if I said one word I would start screaming. I was in the wonderful kind of balance where you can't do one thing that is not right — not for the sake of the other person but for your own sake.

She came in, and I said to myself, "Boy, you watch yourself, because if you say anything, you will tip this thing over, and you are going to have a mess." She was walking around, la-de-da-de-di, and she was touching this piece and pushing that one. She was testing the situation. I was very vulnerable, and I really watched it. I watched every breath I took, and she finally left.

She started coming in every Friday, absolutely every single Friday. This went on for weeks. And I learned every time she came in; I learned tremendously. She was, in a sense, God for me. One day, she was bibbling-bobbling around, doing a whole little scene, when she dropped a bottle. It exploded, and the glass went everywhere. I pulled back and didn't say anything. She started to say, "I'll . . . ," but I said, "No, no. I'll be glad to pick it up." I didn't react. She tried to clean it up and did the best she could, and then she left. I cleaned up the rest of it, and I was very grateful that I had not used her as a scapegoat for the tension in my own inner condition. This is what we do to people who we think are less than us.

She never came back after that. She just walked by. She was calling me "honey" by that time. I would have a store full of people, museum curators and this and that, and I would hear her call, "Hi, honey!" It was very weird, but I understood that she served to make me aware of how precarious my own situation was. I had used her, so then I had to dignify the relationship. And I did, until I dignified it to the point where she was no longer threatened, and she left. But at that point I was sorry that she left, because for me she had become a friend. We grow from these situations; this is using life as a teaching.

Our growth should never be at the expense of someone else or for the price of ridiculing someone else. As we grow we can see that life exists on many dimensions and at many levels. We can see that we are superior in some ways and less developed in others. So, we can look at other people and other situations and stay open, understanding that we have the capacity to take, from everybody, all there is to take and, from everything, what it has to offer.

Certainly if we have to choose what results we would like in life, it is always better to take something that is simple, because it allows us to live quietly with contentment. Simplicity also allows positive things to happen in the area of spiritual work, or metaphysics. It allows our understanding to grow. If we can have simplicity in our growth, we will see the breaking down of the tensions and the resistance to other people, we will begin to see a warmth and sweetness in our lives.

The expression of life is the simple feeling between ourselves and our fellow human beings. Feeling superior intellectually, feeling that we have attained something that someone else has not, is only the expression of evil. The simple nature of life, finally, has to be brought into our ordinary day; it has to be the thing that brings us closer to one another. This allows for the ease of living. It allows for the joy of living. It allows us to look at a child and accept the love that is there. It allows us to take what exists at every moment in this life.

The tensions of our mind and the tensions of our emotions and our wish to be profound always set us apart from everything else. We can't reach, we can't touch, we can't smell, we can't feel because we are so busy being protective of our image. We don't have inside us the nourishment that allows for simplicity.

The greatest moment of my life, the thing that touched me the most, occurred when I was studying in India. I studied with a very great saint, and I watched him go to sleep at night. This man took a potato sack and pulled it in the corner and lay down. It spoke more to me than anything I had ever heard other people talk about. This man was able to sleep simply, without needing a gold and silver bed, without needing all kinds of elaborate external things. He had worked his day and he was able to lie down very simply. It broke about six million muscles in my heart. I saw someone who was giving me peace, who was able to change something in me, and I saw a human being living on the simplest level, doing absolutely the simplest act I ever saw in my life. For me this man was a god, so seeing the simplicity of his act spoke volumes and volumes to me.

I have heard other people talk volumes, and I never saw them perform this kind of action. They were always telling me they were *more* than someone else. They were always involved in expressing their ego and their intellectual capacity, but they never carried out one act of simplicity.

His act of simplicity really reached me. This is what we all need. We don't need some extraordinary concept of a cosmic world. This will come if we have within ourselves the capacity to work and take in more energy. But if we think we are pursuing something seven thousand stories high that is only accessible by a treacherous path, we are really building a tension within our minds that will deny the capacity for this universal consciousness to come into being.

If we don't build nourishment in our life, if we don't build in our day the simple capacity to open to and love our fellow human beings — to see quality in people, to take from people the sweetness that exists in them, to feel the bridge between ourselves and everyone else — we in no way can claim that we have a spiritual life. A spiritual life is supposed to make everyone the same. That sameness comes from loving inside, from feeling within yourself and in another human being this heart, this thing that is God, this thing that needs nourishment. It is not about being more important than somebody else, but about the ability to lower yourself and serve somebody else, so that if they do not treat you in a proper way, you can reach for them and make the relationship right. You can bend, you can be wrong, you can allow yourself to change, you can allow yourself to say that you are sorry, you can allow yourself to have humility.

The arrogance that usually accompanies what we think of as spirituality does not allow for that. It is always right, it is always superior, it is always everything. It does not produce for the other person, who may need nourishment and love, who may need the carpet of life rolled out for them. It places itself above, and I don't believe this is correct.

In the times when I needed help and I received it, there was nothing between me and the person who had this capacity to give. It was given without question. I certainly did not feel worthy, and I was deeply grateful when growth was made possible for me. We have to be sure when we pursue a spiritual life that we are not bringing to that pursuit a

false spirituality

false, negative sense of ourselves that makes us seek to be humiliated, to be stepped on, because we have a need to be suppressed, tortured, and exposed for the person we think we are.

Go where somebody loves you and can only focus on your need for nourishment. Go where someone feeds you and allows you to grow above all the things you find impossible to live with in yourself. You transcend that which you find unacceptable in yourself through the nourishment and love that is given to you.

I had two very great teachers. It was extremely difficult for me to take from them at first, because I felt they were so superior to me. When I tried to express that, I was reassured that the ability to be perfect was not a prerequisite for study. The important thing was the ability to take the nourishment and love that was given, and to grow above myself.

———◆———

In our pursuit of the evolvement of our own creative capacity, we have to have within us a wish for a level that is very much above where we are. This level is only attained by taking in, every day, a higher form of nourishment — not wasting energy, not trying to analyze why we are there, not thinking about all of the things that are none of our business. We should just be grateful that we can take, that there is a place where we can work and a person who wishes to give energy to us, and we should keep drinking this energy in within ourselves and let it flow through chakra after chakra and nourish us in depth.

Every mother who has a child nourishes it without thinking, "Will this child be the president of the United States?" She gives it what she has and then she tries to love it. This makes the child grow. Well, the same thing holds true when you want to grow spiritually. You have to find someone who has that nourishing capacity within him or her, and then you take it in the same way a child takes milk. You drink in the atmosphere in which you are studying, and you take it psychically into yourself.

The result of this nourishment is that you grow more as a human being. You express your growth by breaking tensions and getting above patterns that are detrimental to you. You become freer, you become more open, and you have a sense of joy, a sense of living, and a tremendous sense of gratitude. When this gratitude does not exist in a human being, it is because of ego. We think we have grown from ourselves and are superior to other people. Any human being who is privileged to grow has been given that capacity by many, many other people, and certainly by nature. It is not ours to take for granted, it is not ours to inflict upon other people. Being superior has to do with living in a superior way and being more grateful.

———◆———

We always compare ourselves to other people: they have an IQ of 60, and ours is 80, or we have an IQ of 200, and theirs is 150. But that has nothing to do with the capacity to grow. It is just one barometer. It certainly does not have anything to do with opening, growing, and nourishing ourselves or all the things that life has to offer. IQ, intelligence by itself, does not make a human being happy; it does not make a human being able to feel, to love, to share, to have insight into another person, and to become someone on whom we can depend in every way.

The erratic nature of people is the expression of the limitation of the knowledge that they get. It separates rather than opens them. The simplest expression of spirituality is "God is love." This love is mature energy that ripens and allows us to feel the flow between ourselves and other people. It is the thing that simplifies instead of making tensions and differences, the thing that allows us to feel the humanity we share with another human being. We feel, we care, and we can be involved in a way that is positive; not for gain, but because we have opened ourselves on a human level for the involvement that we are capable of. It is not to get control over somebody else, but just to serve, as one human being should serve another. This is what happens in spirituality when this energy, or life force, flows through a human being: it brings a much more compassionate nature.

———◆———

The only way to be free of pain is to digest it. You eat the pain and you become free. One great

Witch Burning

Growing 31

symbol of that is Jesus being crucified. He was not being punished; he was being freed. You take the crucifixion and you absorb the pain; your physical body opens, and your soul goes out. That is not suffering, it is enlightenment. You have freed yourself. We have read that at the beginning of the war in Vietnam, a Buddhist priest would sit and burn himself alive. Believe me, they did not pull straws to decide who the Buddhist priest would be. They picked someone who had evolved to the point that he would just sit there and burn alive, take in the pain of the burning, and leave his body consciously. You would not hear the man sitting there saying, "Ooh, ooh, it's getting hot." The monk would sit there drinking in the pain and being freed. He would go out with dignity and consciousness. This is the whole difference. The difference lies in being able to take life into yourself and leave karma behind. It is an ability that is not known here, an ability to take life exactly as it is, to absorb it, take the nourishment from it, and rise above it again and again. It is rising above karma — not accepting it, but taking it and eating it.

Somebody who endlessly complains about his or her life will always have to come back and repeat karma. But someone who says, "If God gave it to me, then it must be right, and if I can accept it, then I can surrender it," does not. They eat it up. You can go to a village in India and see that the sweetness and the absolute clarity of spirituality exists there. It is in the very simple people who have accepted life. Their lives may not be pretty and sweet by your terms, but the people there have dignity and freedom, they have

love, and they are open. There is nothing in them that
is closed, they have learned to live their lives with
depth. They have taken everything internally and
they are free. They do not react, because they are
more than accepting of their circumstances. We react
because we do not know the difference; we have not
learned to live consciously with what has been given
to us.

That is what kundalini yoga or any spiritual
practice should do. It should bring us to the in-
evitable point where we begin to take and grow. We
have the nourishment within us, within our own
heart, within our souls; we can open to life and accept
life. That is being practical. It is also being spiritual.
It is being realistic. Spirituality is the only way to
deal with life as it is. Everything else is hiding.

This is a concept that allows you to grow inside, to be more and more nourished inside, and to see
the world as it is. You grow above, you grow stronger
and stronger, because you live stronger. You accept
more responsibility, you become a person who does
not allow yourself to be put down, because you are
grateful. Whatever life gives you, you accept it, and
you grow above it.

The point is not to take the limitation of what
life brings you, but to understand it is all the same
thing, and finally, it is all wonderful. It is full of won-
der; it is full of the energy that can give you extraordinary insight. You have to be able to, inside yourself,
grow and grow and feel this growth as an expression
of love — loving your fellow man, loving life, feeling
the life force coming down, feeling the air and all of

the natural things around you. When you take a drink of water, if you can't feel the water running down your throat inside and be grateful for it, if you can't wash yourself and be grateful for that, then you will never understand spirituality. Spirituality is working so hard that everything is meaningful and everything is wonderful, because it expresses Creation.

The process means finding something that can feed you. You consciously feel something growing inside you. You have more energy, you can break down what was a limitation yesterday. You can draw into yourself and go above the specific situation and see that you are nothing. You have the energy, the nourishment, to see the nothingness of your condition. That is what it is to grow. If you do that every day of your life, you will become free.

Spiritual Work

There is no simple way.
There is only the consciousness of working,
and this takes a tremendous amount of effort.

T he process of growing will take much longer and be much more costly than you think. You are not going to be transformed into great spiritual people unless you work your guts out. It is not going to happen any other way. You are not going to sit in meditation and have enlightenment rain down on you. This I can tell you. You are going to have to sit and work and make sacrifices and work and work and become very effective in your ordinary life. This is an earned thing. It is not given. It is earned. It comes from developing muscles inside, being responsible, and being open. This means you should love the people you claim you love, and be responsible to them. From that you open inside.

A human being is structured just like a Contac™ cold tablet. It is a time-release system. You do so many thousands of hours of work, and something will open in you. I am not kidding. A person has all the mysteries of the universe inside. You work consciously, you collect your energy consciously, and this thing will open in you like that.

He who works will receive. There are no gifts; nobody drops enlightenment on you. You have to work from yourself. You take the energy from somebody who has it, you try to work and find out how to get it in yourself, and it grows for you. But somebody talking up a storm has nothing to do with it. It has nothing to do with talking; it has nothing to do with books. It has to do with muscles within you that you expand and put energy in. You breathe in and collect that energy inside yourself by not wasting it. It collects and grows into something. This takes a lot of discipline and a tremendous amount of perseverance.

———◆———

You have to work, not just sit and meditate. What are you opening to? What are you receiving within yourself? To quiet down your mind and quiet down inside is wonderful. But it is more effective to have something come in that can grow inside you. This thing that comes in is what we call spirit, or spirituality. It is a genuine nourishment, and it is a totally different nourishment than anything on a physical level.

We always grow and grow and grow, and then we rot as people. Everyone talks about growing and growing, then you watch and you see these people slowly rotting away. To grow spiritually is to bloom, it is to have a sweetness develop within you.

If you have a cow that does not give milk, you sell it, if you have a chicken that does not lay eggs, you kill it, and if you have a tree that does not bear fruit, you cut it down. So why should we live without having concrete results every single day?

The miracle of life, the miracle of spirituality, should manifest itself within you, not in promises, but in actuality.

———◆———

Meditation does not mean adjusting to your physical life, becoming passive and tranquil. It means really opening and having a spiritual life. It is a totally different thing. But people use meditation the way a cow eats grass, to quiet themselves down and accept the physical level. Spirituality is to get off the earth. It is not to justify living on the earth and it is not to make the earth a nicer place to live. Understand that you are on the earth for physical reasons, and when you want a spiritual life, you go into a spiritual world.

But you do not jump up off the floor once and think you have made it into the void. You begin to live, your whole system begins to live, in a spiritual world, the world of spirit, which coexists with the world of the physical. And you become deeply responsible for your physical world, because if you are not responsible on the physical level, it will suck you right down from the spiritual realm.

Spiritual life comes out of physical life. When you have perfection on a physical level, when you have an understanding of how to work on a physical level, then you build a spiritual life. But if you think you can build a spiritual life without having a working physical life, you are wrong, because what you are doing is building an illusion. There is no foundation, there is no reality, and there is no consciousness. One thing comes out of the other. From the physical level of your own existence you can give birth to yourself on a spiritual level, just as you were born out of your mother into the physical level.

To grow you have to have a very strong, very solid foundation in life. You have to be able to do everything that life demands of you. Unless you have maturity, you can't commit yourself to anything, period. People who are nuts can't make a commitment to God because they do not have the maturity or the humanity to dedicate themselves to it.

First you have to grow very responsible in the sense that you can work, you can be clean, you can go to sleep on time. Then you learn how to work deeply inside. Otherwise you are just a psychotic surrendering your psychosis to God. God cannot take things like that because that kind of energy does not rise.

I watch people all the time: they meditate and have a little smile on their faces. One thing about spiritual work as opposed to meditation is that in spiritual work you always end up not looking too good because it forces you to see the crap in yourself. People who meditate only see the bliss and the sweetness. In spiritual work everyone else gets the sweetness, and you get the work. It is your service to God. In meditation you live in the sweetness, and everyone else gets the work, because they can't reach you. You are superior, you are removed. But when you are working and serving, and breaking yourself apart doing it, then you really have what makes you free.

———◆———

What is the hardest thing in the world? Reality. Meditation is when you are floating around in your own little spiritual world and you are the ultimate. Reality is when you are working your guts out to stay open so the spiritual force can transcend itself. It is exhausting but fantastic, because you are not caught in the world of your illusion. You are vitally working, you are vitally in contact and you are vitally changing, against your will, against your instinct, and against everything else. Reality has resistance. You are transcending yourself.

Illusion has no resistance. Illusion is fantasy. It is easy — you float off. Our work is kundalini yoga. The kundalini energy can only rise if you are transcending. You have to surrender, then the energy comes up. You have to be constantly opening up so the energy can rise.

There is nothing worse than walking into a room filled with people who have done meditation for ten years. Everyone is superior to everybody else. You can't tell them anything, because they have all the answers. They are totally satisfied; they have a complete, finished thing. It is disgusting, really disgusting. With people who are working, there is no room for talk, there is no room to fight. They are in a state of being, a state of reality. They can't afford to fight with you. They can't afford to even be superior. They can't waste their energy. They are growing.

Meditating is maintaining where you think you are. It is a very egocentric thing. To do our work, you are always breaking yourself down. You see what you are *not*. You are not building ego, and there is no self-satisfaction, because you always know you could have done it better. You could have done it more consciously. You are always learning that you have not done as good a job as it is possible to do. You do not come out a winner, you come out with more work. That is the prize. The only way to win is to end up being free.

———◆———

The work we do is meant to get you the inner energy needed to support you and the area around you. When you do that successfully, the energy will rise in you, because you have your foundation inside yourself. It is a very real and a very practical thing. You have to feel inside you. You have to breathe into your own heart. You can do it once an hour. Just take a deep breath in your heart to feel your heart open. And, if you feel pain in your heart, it is because your heart is closed and you would rather work around it. But you can't work around a chakra. You either go into the center of it and breathe, or you just go into illusion.

Your organs have to be a functioning set of muscles. If your brain is not working, if your heart is not working, if all of the chakras are not functioning, then you are not in a condition to qualify as a human being. All of these chakras represent internal organs that must be alive to hold and spread spiritual force. The chakras have not been perpetuated in the symbols of the Eastern traditions as an amusing thing. They have been preserved for one reason: to show you the inner mechanism that is needed for a human being to have a spiritual life. These are organs that are supposed to exist in a healthy, normal human being.

The energy flowing through these chakras and coming up the spine will give you a bump on top of your head. Then you have a chance for a higher force to come through you. You do not have to be Superman for this bump to appear. You do not have to be completely realized for this bump to appear. Being an authority on one aspect of spirituality does not mean you are enlightened. The word is thrown around with tremendous ease. Everyone is enlightened, but nobody really has love for human beings. So, people teach partial teachings.

I have a long way to go in myself and I am very grateful for it, because it means that I will have a creative life. People who make the claim to be enlightened have only done one thing. They have reached a place where they no longer are capable of growing. So, then they turn other people on. Nobody, until the day he or she dies, qualifies for the title "enlightened being," because somewhere along the way, if you stop working, the circle opens and you begin to lose the quality that has to do with being enlightened.

Plenty of famous painters and great doctors and other people have peaked at age forty, fifty, or sixty and become absolutely second- and third-rate. You have to understand that tendency in yourself. Having qualified one time in your life does not mean that a decade later you will still have that quality. The only way to have a quality that goes on indefinitely is to continually transcend yourself. That means you are growing. You either are growing endlessly or you become an anticlimax.

It is the same with people as it is with products. That is one reason you see everything from a soap powder to a floor cleaner or anything else always being improved on. Everything is always being added to. Universities add courses; General Motors adds new features to a car. Otherwise the products suffer from obsolescence. It is the changing nature of everything. Everything is added to and refined.

Microbiome

Once in a great while somebody will appear who will have a quality that one can appreciate for a lifetime, but this is very rare. If people have that quality it means they are also working tremendously hard to maintain it. It takes an old firm that has been in existence for a long time, like Rolls Royce, to maintain a level of quality, and they have a very hard time doing it. This maintenance does not take care of itself magically. It takes a tremendous amount of work. If you want to have a spiritual life, not only do you have to work inside yourself to attain it, but you have to work to hold it. And, if you are going to work to hold it, you might as well do just a little more work and keep growing. It takes ninety-nine percent of your guts to grow, and it takes an additional one percent to grow twenty times faster. It is this one percent that matters. If you have any intelligence at all, you will make a commitment to go so far beyond where you are that you will have the vitality of growing endlessly.

◆

Ordinary work produces muscles in the body. Physical work, mental concentration, all the things one does in an ordinary day take a certain level of consciousness. If you take care of things on your physical level — you increase your capacity in your job, in your life, with your parents, with the people you are living with or are married to — and you raise your level of consciousness in that area, then your level of spirituality is raised. Someone who is one inch high in their physical life will be two inches high spiritually. If you are a foot high physically, you will be two feet high spiritually.

A very responsible human being making conscious decisions has a chance to become a much higher spiritual being. But a moron sitting and meditating all day and all night is not going to become a very enlightened person. Responsibility is "on earth as it is in heaven." Big on one level is big on the other. If you work more in your life, if you make more effort in your life, if you love people on this level, you can really love God. But if you do not love people, how can you love God? How can you suddenly put into effect, on a finer level, a muscle system that you do not have in place on a coarser, physical level? You can't use spirituality as an escape from the tests and problems of the physical world.

Nobody maintains muscles, whether physical or spiritual, without work, because if you do not use a muscle it gets flabby, and you lose everything you have gained. Through the simple routine of living and working every day, you stretch your muscles, liberating more energy that you can bring through the chakras.

------◆------

Dissolve every tension in your body and you will never have a chance to grow again, but you will be a contented cow. This is what civilization wants; it is what people want. It is like putting chickens in coops so they lay more eggs and the meat is more tender because it does not have any muscle.

Human beings will, I am sure, eventually arrive at the same condition. People think that being retired or working a five-hour day and a four-day week is the ultimate. It is not. It is a twenty-seven hour day that makes for a good spiritual life. You work double time when you sleep. Only working and expanding and taking in more energy and working more brings spirituality.

You have to work, deepen your commitment, expand, and work more. Falling asleep thinking that you are working is wonderful if you are lucky enough never to wake up again. But to wake up one day and find out that you have come down from any attainment that you had is the worst kind of hell. This is what people face, usually in their old age when they realize they have not done a proper job. Your ego can't make a wall thick enough to keep you from the awareness that you have wasted your life, that you have done nothing to use this energy that was put in you.

Energy, finally, is the sacred connection we have with God. We either raise it every day, every moment, and come closer to our realization, or we sit there like a cow looking for a simple way. There is no simple way. There is only the consciousness of working, and this takes a tremendous amount of effort.

———◆———

All you get by working better and deeper is the capacity to work still better and still deeper. It goes against your instinct. You would rather be the dud of the year than the worker of the year. That is all it amounts to.

To have a spiritual life, all you do is become more and more of a worker. And it is important to understand the concept of work: you work deeper, you grow more. A tree that is two-hundred years old has a root system that reaches out for half a mile and draws nourishment out of every little puddle, every little underground stream. Its leaves are reaching and taking in moisture out of the air. An enormous factory feeds nourishment into this great tree. That is how you get strong — you begin to take out of the atmosphere and you begin to absorb the atmosphere around you. You use everything and everybody well.

———◆———

I do not look around inside myself to find the place I always work from and say, "This is the hole where I mine my creative energy. I'm going to work from here." I am not trying to find an easy entry into myself. You start working and you drill fresh. You are drilling through the rock in a new place. You start digging, you start drilling, and you start working. But all of you are looking for a channel, a little place in the rock, a little seam where it is easier and there is less resistance. You become stupid that way.

You have to work your guts out. If you sit down and you find you are made of stone, then you take your mind and you take your heart and you start drilling inside. You want to work and you are going to surrender and you do not give a damn what it costs you. You can stick a piece of dynamite inside. You really work — you talk to yourself and you make believe they put your favorite friend in jail for doing something he is not guilty of. You get furious, you get mad, and you dig and dig and dig, and you demand.

———◆———

When a big shipment of art arrives at my store and we are all working very, very hard, then we have to work very, very hard in our meditations. All this physical activity has to be ground up. The energy you get in your meditation comes from that which you had to transcend in your day. A vital day brings a vital meditation. A dull, boring day in which you try to wish the hours away because you have nothing to do can only give you a dull, boring meditation. One level follows the other.

The Bible says it very clearly: "On earth as it is in heaven." Someone who is an illusionist in life will be an illusionist in their spiritual life. You cannot do rotten, picky, boring work, and avoid working all day long, and sit down and have a good inner life. It absolutely does not happen.

I do not enjoy working as much as I enjoy lying and slobbering around. I am no different than any of you. But I know that when I have worked very hard, then I really enjoy sitting and watching a murder mystery on television or reading a murder mystery. I get a great deal of pleasure out of it. I do not think I can read more than four pages a night without falling asleep. But it is much more real to do that and feel something growing than it is to sit up until four in the morning reading *Siddhartha* and spend the next day dragging around in a stupor. I cannot ever understand that. I always see people who are doing excessive spirituality in certain areas, which makes them completely ineffective in other areas.

I am here only because I need to work hard, not for any other reason. I sit here working inside and try to give you the best that I have in truth and in depth, without any thought of whether you will study with me or not. I am just working, just as any other animal is working.

One constant vision that I had from the time I was eleven to about thirteen — it must have been at least three thousand times — I saw myself as a great ox going around and around a stone, grinding and grinding and grinding all day long. And I realized, "This is what my life is going to be. I am going to work. And work and work and work and work." I am working, and I am grateful, because if I do not work, I will not be able to free myself of the congestion in me. What I am grinding is my tension and your tension, and I am trying to give out a finer energy.

Teacher and Student

A teacher is an instrument through which we draw nourishment and connect to God.

A guru exists to help you, to hold your hand while you are trying to break through patterns. The guru is the midwife. That is all the guru is. This person is the midwife who holds your hand while you are giving birth, over and over again. And this person helps you open to your contact with God. The force that comes through him or her is certainly the force of God, but we need, before we even come to that, reassurance that somebody is going to be there. Then we are ready to give birth.

Nobody has the courage to do it alone. Nobody has the energy to do it alone, and certainly, nobody has the intelligence. This is what a teacher is for. And a student is someone who wants to make that commitment, to hold on night and day, and day and night.

———◆———

Either you are tuned in with the person or you have to sit and wait and maybe never find anything that will work between you and whoever the teacher might be. It is the same as a marriage. It is really a chemistry; it is a chemistry for a particular purpose. To learn from a teacher, and this is true of every teacher who exists, there is the need to tune in, because a teacher is very much like a sending set, and the student is really the receiving set. So you have to feel inside and work around in yourself until you get a frequency that picks up on the teacher.

Almost all people who became spiritual teachers in the past were gifted. This was almost a prerequisite. The great Indian teachers or great teachers in China and Japan that you read about were extraordinarily gifted within themselves. And the greatest demonstration of their gift is that usually when they died nobody who followed them came to the height that they had reached.

It was not that they were trained to that level, or that they evolved into it through a teaching. They had within themselves a capacity that allowed them to grow, evolve, and transcend the level of the atmosphere that they lived in. They were able to extract from nature, from the atmosphere, and from whoever they came to. They had an insight, they were gifted by God, or Creation, they could extract something remarkable out of the atmosphere.

———◆———

My first yoga teacher weighed probably ninety pounds and was ninety years old, but the force coming out of him was so strong for me I actually had to put my hand against the doorjamb and push myself through the door when I walked into the room with him. The energy coming out of him really burned in me. It caused such a tremendous response that after a day or two I had to crawl on my hands and knees, kicking myself along the woodwork, to get myself in. It brought about a tremendous reaction in me, a response that had to do with work, and of course, the response set up a tremendous resistance.

———◆———

It is only a very stupid person, someone who does not wish to grow, who has critical attitudes. It is only someone who has nourishment inside who can open and surrender his or her attitudes and limitations, draw from another person, and learn. I have studied in many parts of the world. And, I have sat with people who I felt were very different from me, and it certainly bothered me. It always bothers us to feel and sense differences. But you learn that you can tune in to somebody, you can develop inside you a sympathetic vibration. You can understand them by having the security inside to open and feel and try to set up a field of energy between yourself and another human being and begin to draw from that person what he or she has to offer. This is, finally, the only way we can grow and the only way we have the capacity to change. Even if we have learned many things, even if we have, spiritually, certain developments, it does not represent the entire capacity that we might have or the entire capacity that exists in the world.

Spirituality is so vast, it is absolutely extraordinary. You can start in one area of a country and go from one place to another, and see that the different teaching expressions all vary enormously. This is a tremendous challenge, because we can only take from what is available. Whether you like the way it exists or not certainly does not change it.

It is no different than taking a course in a university. What a professor teaches may exist in a book, but to extract from that person the knowledge that you want and then, above that, the grade that you desire, requires reaching into the person, understanding his or her psychology, and drawing from him or her — regardless of your own attitude and the resistance you might feel towards that kind of personality. That is spirituality.

Hidden in many people in different parts of the world is a content, a consciousness, that they might or might not be aware of. Taking a gift from another human being does not require that that person be aware of what is being taken. The treasures of the world have more to do with lineages, with the succession of the teachings, than with individual people.

These teachings exist as an energy. And the energy, this abstract quantity, is what we are really after. People always think they can gain learning, knowledge, and wisdom by taking a teaching in words. Words only represent the shell, or the crust, of knowledge. Spiritual knowledge exists in an intangible way. It is drawn off from other people. It certainly is not theirs to withhold. It is ours to take, because spirituality is refined energy that is separate and detached from the person who has that gift, or that capacity. Trying to study them intellectually, trying to dig into their minds, is not the way to obtain knowledge. One can never receive somebody else's secret by trying to pry it out of them, because the more pressure you apply, the more resistance it builds up. But by being open, by surrendering and staying very open in yourself and just drawing within yourself, you will take the nourishment, the energy, from the person, and that knowledge will grow in you.

It is no different than milking a cow. The essence of the energy of a cow is in its milk, and you can draw the nourishment from the cow without having to slay the beast. I have seen so many people go to different parts of the world to study. They come back with an enormous amount of intellectual, or structured, material, but they can't take from that structure the nourishment, or content, that exists within it. The real nourishment — the real wisdom, and the real secret of spirituality, depth, and creativity

— is almost like an invisible energy. It exists separately from a human being. It arises from people's endlessly pursuing a line of work, a line of development. Their conscious effort produces an energy that is detached from them.

You cannot take from that energy on the physical level, where you get involved with them as a teacher or as an institution. If you get involved on that level you get involved with the tensions, you get involved in the politics or the way the institution is structured. You end up being the secretary or treasurer of an organization. You end up working in some kind of a position, rather than just sitting in the atmosphere that allows you to draw the energy inside and evolve.

Finally, structure is always the limitation in any situation because structure is just like a coconut shell — it is the thing that protects the nourishment, the meat and milk of a situation. So, we are growing and allowing our structure to change by taking nourishment, not structure, to put within ourselves.

———◆———

I am, physically, a very strong person. I have had teachers who were very fine and ascetic, sometimes even too refined for me. They were not the type I could relate to easily. I had to sit for two or three days opening and surrendering in myself before seeing them. They were the teacher and I wanted to learn, so I had to sit at their feet, open, and make a great effort. Sometimes this refinement would be very, very difficult for me in myself — in my own psychology, in my own philosophy, in my way of working. I find such overrefinement difficult to relate to. I had to open and open and open until their energy began to contact something in me. Then I could understand them and have some kind of relationship.

There are many approaches to yoga. People will come and say they study with this person or they study with that person. But one teacher does not make another one invalid. What makes a teaching invalid is if it does not work.

A good doctor, when you walk through the door of his or her office, will, ninety-nine percent of the time, know your ailment. As you stand in the doorway they are tuned into you psychically. Then they test you according to what they felt when this communication took place as you walked in. This is very much the nature of teaching; it is very much the nature of magic.

The nature of a commitment to somebody as a teacher is that you stay, regardless of what the outer manifestation is, because what you are interested in is the energy that the person can give you. I once traveled with my teacher to the Himalayas. We traveled with two hippies: one was an American and one was an English boy. They were both pacifists. We stopped at an army camp, because we also had two generals traveling with us, and these kids were going crazy. The situation finally broke when the teacher went into a tank to have his picture taken, and these kids either had to leave or change. They broke and changed.

Anything that happens, any issue that arises, is either a reason to stop working or not a reason to stop working. In my attachment to my teacher, I see absolutely nothing on the right and nothing on the left. I am not concerned with his personality. I am not interested in that. He can do anything he wants to. I know one thing — I am going to hold on for the ride. That way I grow, and I grow tremendously.

Real students are those who can draw this abstract energy within and allow themselves to change by surrendering as this energy expands within them.

I have had students attending my classes who I never even got to know. They came, they took, and they left, and they grew remarkably well. I have had other people who came and became deeply involved. And their involvement became the thing that, more than anything else, stopped their growth, because they made tensions at a greater rate than they were able to take energy.

Taking energy, taking knowledge and learning, can only help a human being if he or she takes and simultaneously digests, absorbs, and grows above a situation. But taking and being involved, getting ourselves dramatically involved, thinking we know, claiming evolvement, and making all kinds of other claims only creates a limitation to the structure of our creative capacity.

———◆———

I so many times came to people who were great teachers. I sat and said, "How is this? How do I deserve to be here?" And they said, "Well, who else is here?" And there were five thousand people there.

I would be sitting there burning because their force was flowing into me. I would be burning and suffering and squirming, and things would be eaten out in me. I was willing to pay the price; somebody else was not. This is what spirituality is about. Are you willing to break down and go up and break down and go up?

The guru represents only the energy contact, the one who removes blocks, not the one who inflicts will and stops you from reaching your realization. And you must know that. Teachers who talk about themselves and their level miss this point. Their level is just a point in space. Physical is here, spiritual is above that, and God is all the way up there. So the guru is just another point. You take yourself and that point, and you draw the line to infinity. If the line stops with the guru, that is a complete limitation; it is a complete cop-out. Somebody has made it to a particular point that he or she is incapable of going beyond; rather than going beyond that point, the person will press you down below the level of his or her development.

God has made us all unique in our potential. The point is to free you to realize your own potential and your own creativity. It is like the water you use to prime a pump. The guru is the water you use to prime your own pump. The guru gives you enough energy to get your own system working, your own creative force flowing.

People who feel bhakti yoga, who have that kind of love for the guru, have an easy way because they are always in love. And love does not necessarily make for work, it makes for acceptance. I do not care for that, myself. I can't stand anyone looking at me with round eyes filled with love, because there is no work behind that. I really do not like it. I do not think of myself that way, and I do not like to be looked at that way. They are absolving themselves of any commitment on their part. They think that I am going to take over all their karma, all their commitments in life.

A human being in any learning situation has to make, inside, the commitment of growth. Growth brings about resistance. It is your problem, with anyone you study with, to overcome that resistance. And it is the continual transcending of the resistance that gives you your enlightenment. Just feeling resistance means you have an energy force that is working against you. If you surrender, you absorb that energy force, and it will give you your enlightenment. So you have, immediately, within the fight itself, the solution.

———◆◆———

A teacher is not to be honored. A teacher is an instrument through which we draw nourishment and through which we connect to God. So we should always open to him or her and then go up and reach. We should not be limited by the person, but, because of the person, be able to find a higher quality and

quantity of energy and flow. This is the way you are
nourished from it; it is the way you nourish me. But
the sterile, limited idea of what we are and what somebody has to offer becomes our limitation, because we
do not have the courage to surrender deeply inside.

———◆———

When I can't feel with any one of you, love
you, and feel every muscle in my body relate to you
and want to nourish you, it is not a lack in you; it is a
lack in me. But as a result of what has been generated
in this culture for the last few thousand years, everyone has to approach teachers like one peasant approaching another peasant or a buck approaching a
doe. You have to do a kind of ritual dance to get them
to love you. But they should be in a condition where
they are able to love you because they are nothing in
themselves. The thing that stops love, the thing that
stops energy flow, is only one thing — it is having
chemistry that has personality. Chemistry should be
able to function on any level and for everybody, because a true teacher should be a true servant.

———◆———

You can always receive more by having more
of an opening in yourself. The greater your surrender,

of course, the more the flow will go from me to you. I can't not give to you. But you can take more, because by being empty inside, you create a vacuum that will draw out more from me. And a vacuum does not take place in a human being whose mind is busy analyzing, questioning, doubting, and all these other things. These are things that fill us. We are filled with ourselves. We are filled with our egos. The less open the person is to receive, of course, the more destroyed the psyche is and the more protected he or she has to be. When you have nothing to protect inside of you, when you really are free to expose yourself, it means your ego can dry up and your soul is free to open.

There is no loyalty to any teacher if you are beneath the level of the teacher's existence. To be a good Christian and love Jesus is to use the energy of Jesus to grow beyond. He freed himself. You are here to free yourself. You should not be limited by Jesus, the Buddha, or any teacher, because they are nothing more than the servant of God, or the servant of higher creative energy. In no way, shape, or form should the teacher become a limitation for you. There is no teacher that is any more than a servant of God. And you do not ever, if you go to a good house, get involved with the servants. You let them serve you so you become freer. Anyone who ever tells you they are God or they are more than God, is revealing his or her own paranoia. You don't have to pay attention to that. You can even absorb that. You take in energy and transcend the situation.

———◆———

When people start telling you that what they are doing is for you, then you have to be careful. Anyone who really teaches, who really has anything to do with you, should be doing it for themselves. It should be for their own growth.

I will never take a student if I do not feel that his or her being with me is of prime importance for me. Why else should I have the student there? If it is not valuable for me, in my own growth, to have you here, you absolutely should not be here, because then you are a parasite taking energy from me for no real reason. You have to exist as an expression of my growth, as an expression of my attachment to God, and as an expression of my capacity to be detached from you.

———◆———

To survive a teacher takes an extraordinary type of disciple. You have to be a brilliant disciple to survive studying with almost anybody, because teachers generally have a need to bind you to them. I knew an old man who once said this about going to the hospital. He said you have to be very strong to go to the hospital, which is true, because the treatment in the hospital is so bad, the food is so terrible, and there are so many germs that it takes all your strength to survive it.

The attachment inflicted on people spiritually is so terrible because it takes them away from the opportunity of being free and being realized. Realization comes from attachment to God, not attachment on the physical level.

Practice

Feel the life force flowing from you and drawing into you from the atmosphere: from the rain, from the sky, from the air around you and the sky above you, and the stars and the moon and the sun, and everything that exists that represents energy.

T his is the exercise: take a breath through your nose, swallow in your throat, let the air come into the heart. Feel the expansion taking place for the count of six, ten, or fifteen, until you feel an opening in your heart. Then slowly exhale about one-fifth of the air, or else exhale to the count of six or ten. At this point, the air and the energy start expanding in the heart, and you feel the expansion. Take a second breath, and the accumulation in your chest will be knocked down by the breath into the lower, abdominal chakra. The energy will come down and start to expand in this lower chakra. Keep your attention there until you feel the energy expanding and expanding and expanding, again for the count of six, ten, or fifteen, as you wish. You will feel the muscles moving.

As these muscles open, energy is freed. This energy will sometimes go into the sex chakra, or you may feel a little burning or tension on the base of your spine. If so, then rotate on the base of your spine; the energy will come up your spine and gather at the top of your head. Keep a sense of openness in this lower chakra as this is going on. Then try to keep drawing energy from me, or if you are sitting in your house, use a photograph or just try to draw the energy that is in the atmosphere. Keep feeling this mechanism open.

After you have done this for some months, you can take one breath and feel it go all the way down inside you. Some people have done a lot of pranayama or are naturally gifted that way, so they may take one breath and feel the energy open them completely. The exercise is not meant to restrict you; it is a means to work with whatever natural talent you have. Some people are very, very tight inside. They may have to breathe much more in their chest. They may have to take several breaths in a row.

If you do not feel the expansion, then keep working until you do, because it is useless to assume anything. You either feel this thing open or else you sit for an hour and hold your attention inside. You take a breath and keep your attention there, trying to feel something. If you feel a little stimulation, a little movement, fine. But if one day you feel it open up and the next day you take a breath and it is like pouring water on a rock, nothing will happen. Keep working until this heart opens. Unless that chakra is open, what is the use of going on to the next one? When you feel your heart opening, it is an energy in the heart that is starting to flow. Then you take the next breath into the heart, which brings the energy down to the abdomen, and you will feel it expand. Then you carry it through the sex organs and up the spinal column.

A lot of things that will come up if you come to the classes are not rational in the normal sense, because spirituality has to do with spirit, it does not have to do with the physical. So some of the things you will do, although they are not rational, have great rational quality as far as spiritual work is concerned, because they work. One of these things has to do with the throat chakra, which people very rarely understand.

That is why in our exercise we always talk about a double breath — you take a breath, you swallow in the throat, and you let the air come down into the heart chakra. The swallowing of the air is to activate the throat chakra. On the second breath, you breathe in again, and the breath liberates something in the chest, and the energy comes down to the area below the belly button.

A way of expanding that energy is to swallow. You just make believe you are swallowing something in your throat. You can do this between the double breathing. You do the double-breath exercise maybe five times in a half hour, but a lot of times you may not be able to get enough energy to flow, so you take a breath, or just swallow in your throat a few times — it has a remarkable capacity to expand the force in your chest or in the lower chakras. Also, you should always try to keep some of your attention on your sex chakra and the tip of your spine. The minute you feel any energy or warmth in those areas, rotate just a little bit on the base of your spine to bring the force up the spine. Then your neck will always move.

Try to be sure you are not tense, because all of these tensions are energies that will keep the flow from taking place. They will send the force outside you. You want to internalize all this energy. You want to make a flow that increases inside. The flow should not be like a shoelace; you shouldn't feel a little, tiny flow going down and a little, tiny flow going up, because you are not going to be reborn a worm. You want to be reborn complete. So feel this energy flowing right through your whole chest and beyond you. Every chakra should extend beyond the physical size of a human being. You feel the flow coming through all of you.

If you breathe a little slower — you take one breath in and hold it a little longer — you feel more and more and more and more open in you. The energy becomes a big flower instead of a little tiny flower. It has a bigger opening.

───────◆───────

I draw on your chemistry because you all represent the shock absorbers for me when I go to another level. You should, in your own growth, take and use me the same way. This is what a spiritual class should be. Those of you who really want an extraordinary spiritual life can use me and everyone else in the room. That is what a pool is for. It is what a collective pool of brains is for in a laboratory. It is what a collective group of people are for in a university — the advantage of a great quantity is available for any individual with the capacity to dig in and use it.

———◆———

Any experience or vision you have, just drink it in as force. Bring it up your spine and forget it. You do not keep a diary in your mind of what happened. You never try to relive a previous class another time. You never do that. It should be fresh all the time and it should be vital all the time. And the quantity you get or the quality you think you get is absolutely unimportant.

The essential thing is that you work until you absolutely can't work any more. You should really work and have a sense of vitally working against resistance. You are opening more and more and more; you have a great sense of doing, a great sense of expansion, and your mind is inside feeling these muscles opening, feeling the energy expand. Like a bee gathering honey, you are moving to each chakra, freeing a force in each one. The flow of it brings it down through the sex organs, up the spinal column, allowing you to harvest it at the top of the head.

You really are gathering your life force with your consciousness. That life force accumulates at the top, and then it ripens. Then your life force secretes another energy that comes from the crown of your head right into the brain. Until you feel that, you are having an isolated experience. If you get caught in the mystical event, you become a human being involved in external expressions of spirituality instead of one who is using all of that energy internally to become free. You get lost in the Madame Blavatsky kind of experience. You see the Buddha, you talk to Kuan Yin, or you are involved with Krishna.

You have to realize that any externalized manifestation, whether it is a physical form or a spiritual form, is nothing to be involved with. It exists for you to be freed by it.

———◆———

If you have a problem, you ask a teacher about it. If you have to go over it, you go over it. And if you still do not feel it working, then you ask again. You have a right for it to work. There is no reason in the world it should not work for you. If it does not work, then you come and you bother me. You are not here to be polite. You are here to get results. You are here not to look spiritual, but to really have a spiritual mechanism opening and working. There are times when you will be sitting, not doing anything except being open. You will then join in the Om sound.

For those of you who do not know what the Om sound is, the sound of Creation, or the Atman, the energy coming into the atmosphere, it is like the very resonant sound you might hear when you pass a telegraph pole or any electrical wire carrying energy. It is a very fine hum, like an electrical sound vibrating. You try to draw that in through your head and into your system. It is the energy of God, the energy of Creation, coming into our universe. And, you try to be open to it. Even when you are walking, try to take a breath and feel yourself open to the energy in the atmosphere so that you draw this energy into yourself.

———◆———

Who says spiritual work, or any kind of conscious work, has to be anything but a lot of fun? It does not have to be a serious, dogged kind of thing. You should enjoy it. You should have a sense of drama. You should have a sense of vitality. And you should, more than anything else, have a sense of the endlessness of it. It does not have to be *one* way. You do not have to sit there in a position you saw in a movie picture; that is not necessary. It is like riding a wave in Hawaii. If the wave comes at different angles, do you always go the same way? You gauge the flow of energy and you surf that way. You know how to jump it, you know how to ride it, and you know how to keep on top of it.

This is what spirituality is about. You learn the direction of the energies that are coming into you. You work with it, you study it, and then you go out and have a great day. Regardless of what is coming in, your day will be great; it will be dramatic. You become one with this flow of energy, and you make a very good day for yourself. It is not a matter of sitting there saying, "Oh, what does my astrology chart say? Today isn't a very good day, I have to lock myself in the closet. This negative force is coming in." That is ridiculous.

It is all in the way you ride your day. You must ride it creatively by knowing what you have to work with. Then you dress accordingly and you act accordingly. But if you try to fight a force that is coming in one direction — you want to go to the right and the force is coming in from the left — you are going to get smashed. You are going to get pulled into the undertow. You have to work along with the direction of the energy for that day. Lying in bed in the morning, feeling the energy come in, feeling the direction of it, feeling your attitudes, you know what you have to do.

———◆———

In everything you do, you have to feel a love and a connection. You have to feel you are doing something because you want to do it, and you want to do it because it increases the flow and connection between you and life. It is a living connection, not a thing you do like a blind man tapping his way down the street. You are choosing to do whatever it is even if you do not like it. You are choosing to do it; you really make it your choice.

It is the same way with your coming to class. If I did not want you to come, you would not be here; it is my choice. As long as it is my choice, then it is up to me to love you all the time and make the effort to connect with you. That is the only way it should be: I dignify you when you come here with my feeling of attachment to you, and you, in turn, as someone who was chosen to come here, who has been accepted, should also dignify your presence by being here as a person who comes out of choice. It should exist that way; it should be mutual.

You are not stuck with me. I am not your uncle, your father, your brother, your mother, or someone you have promised to do something for. You are a human being who is coming here consciously. If you do not come here every time with that inner attitude, your ability to take, your ability to assimilate, your ability to grow from it becomes less.

<hr/>

To sit in class in your head like a jackass, over and over again, represents the most inconceivable stupidity that it is possible for you to come to. It really means one thing: you absolutely do not give a damn. You have to realize that. You may not even give a damn, but you have to have a sense of craft, if nothing else. If you are not capable of caring enough for yourself then you have to be, at least, respectful of your responsibility to perform this spiritual act, which is to really flow and function. If you do not care for yourself, then you certainly should not be in class, because you represent, then, an obstacle, not only for yourself, but for everyone else in the room.

This is the part you should become increasingly aware of. You are responsible. You are absolutely responsible when you are here, not just for yourself, but for everyone around you. And either you take your breath, go inside, and open, or you have no right to be here. If you want, you can express your lack of wish, your lack of commitment to your spiritual life. That is fine — then stay in your own atmosphere. When you bring yourself into an atmosphere where other people are trying to grow, then your responsibility extends beyond yourself. It extends to everyone around you. And then, dammit, you better work, because if you don't, I'll throw you out.

This is the important part of a commitment to a group. It is just like what people do professionally. Whether you work as a pilot on a plane or as an employee of a large organization, your particular piece of work does not begin and end with you. It is part of a whole, and you do not have the right to ruin the whole.

———◆◆———

Spiritual work is spirit. It is bringing in higher and finer forces to impregnate us. When you sit there with your heaviness, with your self-pity, with your stupidity, with your ineffectiveness, then you are not only contaminating the atmosphere around you, but you are helping to sustain the tremendous negativity that exists on the earth.

This is because ignorance breeds ignorance, and a lack of spirituality in you helps breed a lack of spirituality on the earth. It is vital that your commitment be to yourself, your own refinement, and the atmosphere around you, while your attachment is to God, or higher creative energy. So, when you sit, you have to be inside. You have to be open before you come to sit here. You have to have had, on your way here, this sense, this feeling inside. Really feel the life force flowing from you and drawing into you from the atmosphere: from the rain, from the sky, from the air around you and the sky above you, from the sun, the moon, the stars, and everything that exists that represents energy. Feel that you are consciously drawing energy in and letting your inner being be nourished by that.

———◆———

If you begin to feel something when you meditate, and you consciously breathe then, you will be spreading the energy of the experience with your breath. This is taking one level of consciousness and expanding it with another level of consciousness. You are using air. This is pranayama, which is absolutely essential, not only for yoga, but for any kind of spiritual work. You are taking the one thing that you need to live and using it to live spiritually.

Swami Nityananda always said if you do not give a man food for two weeks, he can survive; if you do not give him water for a week, he can survive; but if you do not give him breath, he can't survive. Breath is the most sacred of all the things we take. It is the one we need and can't live without for any period of time. That is the secret. You can't live without breath. Then, certainly, if you can expand your breath, if you can use your breath consciously, you can have a much more extraordinary spiritual life. Without breath, you cannot have a spiritual life. It is totally impossible.

———◆———

Every conversation should be made subservient to your inner condition. To talk to anybody and not have this flow inside you only reflects ignorance and a lack of consciousness. Come back to the exercise, which can be as simple a thing as taking a breath. Just one single breath can lift you enough above a situation to stop you completely and change your understanding, because one breath is detachment.

It is the same as a bullet coming at your head: just move out of the way a little bit and it won't strike you. All the talking, all the work you do, is nothing unless you have within you the capacity to make this slight movement.

————◆————

All the time, when people get desperate, they ask me, "What do I do and how does it work?" It has nothing to do with me. It does not even have anything to do with them. It has to do with the simple act of breathing.

The whole effort of pranayama and yoga is based on being able to take a deep breath and consciously expand inside, so all the work, all the muscle structure you have created, all the creative inner mechanism you have put into effect can function. It is no different than buying a car and taking care of it, and then forgetting to put fuel in it — it will not operate. What you need to operate your spiritual system is, more than anything else, to remember to take a breath and have this energy open and start the mechanism running in you. It is as simple as that.

————◆————

I read something that Nityananda wrote about breath that was very beautiful. He said, "To breathe in deeply is like feeling a bucket going down a well." So I took a breath and could feel it going all the way down. It really was like a bucket. It is amazing: you can hear it splash when it hits you someplace below the belly button. It is a wonderful feeling. You try and take a breath now. It is like hearing a bucket clanking on both sides as it goes down, and it takes much longer to splash than you think it should. This is because you are much deeper as a person than you think you are.

This has nothing to do with a quick breath in and out. If you can breathe that way, then you can take a deep breath in and really feel the bucket knocking back and forth on its way down. It works its way down, you feel it hit, and you feel the expansion that breathing can bring to your system. Then you let the air out, and the air takes out the poisons from within your system.

A breath like this is not a breath that can happen unconsciously. It only happens with your consciousness. You have to have your mind and your brain following this bucket of air as it goes down through your system. It is wonderful, because once you can picture it, you never take a breath consciously again without feeling this whole process.

———◆———

Everything outside you is a manifestation of God that you have to transcend. You have to look at things objectively. Nothing is real except your ability to transcend a situation through your conscious will and your breathing. This is all that exists. The other will disappear like snow on a hot street the minute you look and say, "I will withdraw from the situation. I will detach myself because this situation is nothing more than a test of my capacity to live above it."

The point is not to meet the situation head on. If you meet it head on, you are stuck in your mind. But if you take a breath and you start consciously opening up — if you do the exercise you have been given over and over again here — you pump yourself full of energy instead of letting your energy go out, bleeding into everything and everybody. If you bring your mind, your breathing, and your energy inside and you keep working inside, slowly but surely you rise. As a phoenix rises from its own ashes, you rise out of the shit in yourself and transcend yourself.

———◆———

When you wake up in the morning and are lying there, you have to within yourself say, "Well, what will I be today?" A little moan will come out of you. You take a deep breath in your heart, and you feel your heart does not want to move. If you stop the moan, take another breath, start priming the pump, and start working, you will work yourself out of the stupid level you find yourself in. Keep breathing until your heart opens. Then take a shower and you should start laughing.

———◆◆———

I do not want to be looking in somebody's window saying, "I wish I could buy that." I work, I open, and I do. This is your own situation, too. You want, you do. Nobody can stop you if you really want. The only person who can stop you is yourself. You just have to be able to gauge your state by your breathing and your feeling inside. See if you can't feel your heart beating and opening; feel the energy coming through your sex organs. It should always feel like champagne bubbles. That is the only feeling I would accept. The energy of your life is coming through your sex organs and being transformed into higher spiritual energy. You are a factory. You are a factory walking on the earth. Your raw material is physical energy that has to be transformed continuously into spiritual energy.

This is a living human process. It is what a plant goes through. A plant takes in one kind of energy and transforms it into another. If you use your conscious will, you can carry the creative energy through your sex chakra and make it recreative energy. You can make it spiritual energy. You then become a spiritual person. You are consciously responsible for the energy that flows in your body. And that is what our work is about.

Try sometimes to do this when you are walking along the street. Just take a breath and try to visualize your heart opening and opening and opening. Feel a oneness. Instead of being limited by you, the energy can spread beyond your physical body. And this is true of all the chakras, all the spiritual and psychic muscles. They are larger than life-size. They in no sense should be limited to your physical self, because they express the energy of God or higher creation. When you limit this energy within yourself, you create a paranoia, because this force is trying to expand in a limited area. It becomes more and more pressurized. You can drive yourself crazy this way. But if you can surrender the energy so that it extends out beyond you, you become very generous with it. You let this thing become very extraordinary.

When somebody comes into my shop as a customer or as a student, they are a connection between me and life. When I look at them that way, it immediately makes a greater flow possible. And if I do not feel that I am in a good condition, if I feel the tensions of the day, then I say to myself, "Baby, you

are not as qualified right now. Don't inflict your condition on that person."

So you begin to judge your own capacity at
any given time, and you connect in spite of the way
you feel. You learn to transcend your own chemistry,
to transcend the tension of the day, so you bring life.
You relate in such a way that you do not connect on
the lowest level, but on much higher levels. Say you
look at a person and you instinctively dislike him or
her — you are reminded of your mother, your father,
your grandmother, or an uncle who hit you. You look
at the person and say, "He is like John or Uncle
Frank." Then you look again and say, "No, what do
they have that I can relate to? I don't want to be stuck
with John; I don't want to be stuck with Uncle Frank."
You try to find something in you that can relate to a
higher level, not to the lower level of the situation.
You try to feel a flow of life.

If you find aspects of them that remind you of
other difficult situations, then you just completely put
those situations to the side, because you are not going
to tune in on that. If you do not tune in on it, it does
not exist. If you nourish something that is loving,
that has flow, that is healthy, it has to come to life. We
immediately set in motion a connection between ourselves and someone else.

———◆———

Anybody can look at a painting or a work of
art and complain about it. You can say, "Lookit, the

feet are big, the hands are big, the nose is this way, and why does it have those ears?" You can pick and pick and pick. Well, a work of art should not be in any way touched by the mind. It should be a flow of energy. You look at it and feel the beauty of it, you feel the life of it, you let it carry you.

You should become aware of a human being the same way — a person is a flowing, creative force. You relate to that instead of picking and picking and picking. Do not forget, it is a crazy human being who needs perfection. The closer you are to evolvement, the less perfection you need.

When somebody comes into my store and they want to spend $25, they really want a plastic Buddha they can rub with Brillo wire. They want it to be clean, and this and that. The nick on the ear, on the nose, or anywhere else — it annoys them. They are vulnerable! The more vulnerable you are, the more perfect you need something to be. The crazier you are, the less rational you are in yourself, the more you demand from somebody else. But God does not demand anything from anybody. God symbolizes the level of perfection that encompasses everything. The higher the energy, the more *it* can complete everything.

So in the realm of art, you take a torso. It can sell for $50,000. But someone who is a connoisseur will look at that chest and back and they will see the whole statue. They will see more than the whole statue — they will see every Greek and Roman head that ever was. They will get more than they paid for. They will not see the limitations. They will see it without limitations, because they know the art.

When you become aware of the art in a human being, the creative flow in a human being, you really do not need much. There is so much to love, there is so much beauty, there is so much flow, there is so much perfection, there is so much of a wonderful nature to relate to that you do not have to pick at all of the small things. It is your bigness that makes everything beautiful. It is the vastness of the flow within you that finishes off all the chips and the broken parts and the limitations.

People who pick and pick and pick are neurotic. They are without love.

———◆———

This is the attitude you should have with other people: they are not the enemy. That out there is not the enemy. It is a test for you to open to and feel the connection with.

We have to serve each other, which means we are serving God and serving energy. We are connecting with energy and evolving with energy. Treating everyone as if they were antagonistic and hateful and trying to get you is an expression of an insane human being. The need you have to fight and fight and fight for hours and days exists because you do not want to open and flow up.

There is nobody who does not give you during the course of a conversation, regardless of their condition, a hundred ways of taking energy and moving up with it.

———◆———

Right before I closed my store one night a woman came in. She was wearing a coat with a piece of fur off here and a crack there, and the dark roots of her dyed hair were about six inches long. She priced a piece, and the piece was very expensive. Then she started telling me that somewhere else the things were much cheaper. Well, she happened to pick one of the most expensive pieces in the store.

Now, I had had a day that was not very easy, and I looked at her and started picking her apart in my head. I looked at the coat, I looked at the roots, I looked at the little squeezed face. I looked at this and I looked at that. Because of what my day had been like I was taking my identification to that level. I was putting a block between me and her, not just because of the piece and her attitude, but because of a need in me. Then I could feel myself not only judging her, but, inside myself, oppressing her. So I took a deep breath and I turned it around, because it was not fair. That woman had signs on her face of a great number of things she had gone through that were not very happy. And I was using the fact that everyone was jumping on me to justify my jumping on her.

I turned it around inside, and I opened. Then I showed her another piece that was $450, and we talked a little bit. Then she said she was not really in the mood to buy. But she was graciously, and perhaps unconsciously, rising up a little bit, to the point where she was talking about the possibility of coming back. It did not matter to me whether she came back or not; it just was not right for me to have those bad manners with her.

Finally we talked a little more and she priced two or three things. Then, pointing to a piece, she asked, "How much is that?" And I said, "Well, that's $1,000." And she was kind of easing up, because *I* was easing up in myself. As I was opening to her I was watching her rise up in herself. Then she said, "Well, I'll only take it for $500." And I thought, "Well, I have injured you in myself. I have injured you fifty percent of the situation at least." I said, "I'll give it to you but for a very strange reason. It's because I feel I owe you an apology."

I was grateful in myself to be able to open, realize I was wrong, and give in to her and to the situation, because she in no way deserved the way I was psychologically treating her. We ended up being a little friendly, and we talked for a few minutes.

I had turned around in myself, which prepared me to have a good class. If I went home with that situation badly resolved, I could not teach a decent class.

You begin to, in a real way, say you are sorry, not because of a difference between you and another person, but because you are using your energy in a wrong way. The point is to open; it is to open a situation, to reach into somebody and open.

———◆———

In tension there is an abysmal stupidity, an abysmal lack of intelligence. It is very easy to correct somebody, and by correcting them you press your judgment into their tension. They did not mean what they said. They did not in any way mean it. What happens is God is talking through them in what we think is a negative way. And they are saying, "I've made this mistake, can you give me energy, can you love me in spite of my making a wrong decision, in spite of my not doing the perfect thing?"

Who is perfect? You can have a perfect action. You can have a perfect response that is a much higher level of response than that of your ordinary self. Because you have become conscious, you make a move that has awareness in it, that has love in it, that has understanding, that has surrender and that, more than anything else, acknowledges that you are a jack-ass. You do not have to be right. You can surrender this thing that instinctively expresses tension. And you pull back, finally, because you know, after sixty million times, that you can take a breath and separate a little bit. You say, "Look, maybe I don't see it right." You detach enough to look at the situation objectively. Then you say, "Is the action, is the movement, is the quantity coming from me going to go into the person and make something live for me or will it be a suspicious thing, a mind thing, or an emotional thing?" We have, finally, that choice.

———◆———

Surrender is a muscular thing. Say you have a fight with your wife or a fight with somebody else.

You sit down. Inside you, what is going on? You want to be right. "I'm a nice guy, how could this person do this to do me? How could someone take advantage of me in the business world," or "How can somebody not love me? Don't they understand what I did?" Inside you, these muscles close up; they are protecting you. They are protecting your ego, protecting the image you have of yourself. You sit down to take your breath, and you find that something has robbed you of your heart. What robbed you of your heart? The need to be right.

These muscles do not want to open. They would rather you were safe and secure behind the wall than outside the wall. Surrendering is opening all the muscles. This is the real test of your surrender in a situation. Can you breathe? Does the throat open to receive the energy? Are you free to receive this energy and open and see what your condition really is? If you find out you are constricted in your heart, you have a pain in your back, or you can't get the air down, what does it mean? It means you are closed. What closed you? It does not matter what closed you, you do not have to find the rational reason, you just have to open. You sit and work, and you breathe.

I do not have that problem anymore, but I used to sit and take that breath six hundred times in one day, sometimes, to begin to feel a little crevice start to open. If you are closed, you are dead. You can't be right if you are closed. Can a closed person know what he or she did or did not do? So, if you find that you are closed, you have to drop the whole issue of whether the other person is or is not right.

We have the only spiritual mechanism in the world that has got a safety valve on it. If this thing is not open and flowing, then you are in trouble.

Tension

Tension is nothing more than energy under pressure. It is very strong spiritual food.

T he thing we basically suffer from is a lack of awareness of what we are involved in, which is life. Life has a quantity, a quality, and a density. Our lack of awareness, our unconsciousness of it, allows us to use it improperly.

For that reason a silt of unassimilated energy and unassimilated consciousness builds up in a human being every day. There is nothing profound about this; it is the simple outcome of a product that is not being used properly. Life is a product. It is a conscious, creative quantity. And we are guilty of reneging on our responsibility to it. By not being open to it we allow it to drop in us some dust, some unassimilated creative energy, every day. This dust builds up and buries us. It is this very quiet, deep silt of unconsciousness that really destroys a human being. We get deeper and deeper and become completely covered by this energy.

We have no way of dealing with it except through a spiritual capacity that allows us to rise above our day, to assimilate the energy of our day, and to break down in ourselves the by-products of the energy we use in relating to the world and relating to other people. Because of the quietness with which this silt accumulates, it does not provoke a drama. We are not inspired to do anything about it, and it just quietly builds up. After a week or ten days when we have not worked properly, when we have not flushed from ourselves the tensions of living, when we have not assimilated the consciousness of the energy in which we are moving, we start to become dulled. We then reject ourselves because we are not using our life for the purpose for which it was made.

Deeply within us, underneath all the silt, is the consciousness of life, something that really does know better. It begins to form disease, it begins to form other kinds of malfunctioning that are only the efforts that the healthy body and healthy mind underneath all this uses to express to us the need to do something. But instead of being provoked to a conscious effort, we go out and have ourselves cut and mauled and psychologically taken apart. We do not do that which is within us. We do not do what we are capable of doing, which is to live in a deeper way.

Life, taken consciously, produces an inner sense of vitality and well-being. When we do not work correctly, when we do not relate correctly, everything in us tries to tell us. We feel pains, tensions, dullnesses. All of these things speak from within us to show that we are rejecting ourselves, we are attacking the people whom we should love. We in no way can become a vehicle for life; we can't nourish what we are responsible for.

We build blocks and thicknesses, which is exactly what we are trying to break down by doing conscious work. With our own breathing, which is the simplest and most obvious of all methods for reaching something inside, we draw in the energy of the atmosphere and try to remove the blocks that exist within us. It is not a dramatic effect that we are working for. All the movements that go on in class only represent energy being taken into muscles that are almost dead. When you feed them, they start to make these little spastic movements. It is for the purpose of this feeding that we need the consciousness to open to, and be quiet and easy with, this energy.

Human beings have the capacity to live like the simplest animal. If they live in a simple atmosphere, they can thrive and have inside them that which every human being is entitled to — peace of mind and a sense of well-being. But the minute you take a human being into a more complex atmosphere, the tensions on the outside produce something on the inside that makes for the rejection of life, the closing off of different vessels, the closing off of muscle, the closing off of blood and circulation and air.

We are living in an atmosphere, this city, which is very dense and compacting, so our conscious effort must increase to compensate for the tensions around us. But this is not a bad thing. It is the most wonderful place in the world to live because the effort it requires will make us the strongest of all people. We get strong by living a strong life, by consciously accepting our role with the understanding of its purpose and with love and gratitude for the opportunity there. To sit in the country where there is no demand, no potential, no competition, is useless. It is almost impossible to work without tension, without something to overcome within yourself.

But with all these natural opportunities around us, we suffer because we can't make a simple effort. We can't do what is needed to raise ourselves above all this silt and smog. We continually complain about that which is really our gift of life. It is something that gives us the capacity to grow very strong. A creative life, which is certainly equally available for every human being, is the ability to put the total person in a situation that tests his or her capacity. But we continually compare our situation to somebody else's. It becomes an endless stupidity. It is the individual facing his or her individual test. You can't possibly learn by seeing the way somebody else works, by seeing somebody else's abilities or limitations. It is our individual connection with our creative source of energy that is important.

We must become aware that our ability to grow is a technique that we learn. This is what you are here for: to learn a technique that can allow you to milk life — not just one way, but eventually every way. You grow strong and go out and take from life its content on every level. The point is not to worship one person or be involved with another or be under somebody else's tension, but to become a free human being who can take and take.

But we have a need to over-identify with the sources from which we take, from the sources we make essential for our life. We are so busy squeezing that we are not eating and growing and transcending. Our whole life is filled with complicated symbols, because our life is not filled with the essential simplicities that allow us to go through life accepting the goodness and beauty that is there. If we can keep our lives less complex, then when we come to something more, something wonderful, we can appreciate it because of the ease with which we are given, the simplicity with which we receive it, and the freedom that it gives us.

We inflict a life of tension and limitation on ourselves because we cannot find within ourselves gratitude for living. Our lack of gratitude for our existence, for our life as it is given, forces us to make tensions just like a child throwing a tantrum. We continually exercise our will to show how unacceptable it is, and we forget to take what is available. It is this unconsciousness that keeps people in a ridiculous state of starvation. They are busy making tensions instead of taking the very simple quantity that can free them, that really represents love and nourishment and growth.

Some of you are here for a very simple reason: just to take a little more, to eat a little more, and to be freed a great deal so that you can take from your own environment, from the atmosphere of your own life, that which you are entitled to.

Consciousness is understanding that tension is the game of wasting energy, of not clearing yourself out on a day-by-day basis, of not recognizing the difference between something that does not nourish you and something that does. The reason for growing becomes evident as you do it, because the energy you gather within yourself has within it the capacity to explain to you the purpose of your life. But we do not hear the language of life because we are continually involved in the language of death, which is tension, fighting, and all of these negative things.

Life is complete. It can impart life to us whenever we have the capacity to be open to it. It is the great simplicity in which we live. And yet we destroy that simplicity by almost every act of our existence. We can't open inside and let the energy pour into us. The whole atmosphere is loaded with this energy, yet we have to come to an ashram or monastery under special conditions to get our system back to a point where it can exhibit this simplicity in its ordinary day under either ordinary or extraordinary conditions.

So when you really try to work and you try to grow, what you are doing is simply using your ability to take nourishment and not make tensions that destroy the nourishment you are taking. Otherwise you will spend the next six million years doing this thing that is basically very simple. It is feeding yourself, releasing tensions, and becoming free.

It is essential for all of us to understand that spirituality is just the releasing of spirit by feeding nourishment into tensions. What could be simpler? Underneath the tension is an extraordinary mechanism that has the capacity to instruct you. It has its own voice, it has its own intelligence, and it certainly shows you, when you treat it correctly, what it can do. It is no different than having a child express by its tantrums that it is not happy. We have to learn that this thing within us is another kind of a child. When we feel something that is not easy for us to identify, we have to just stop for a second, detach, and try to understand what is wrong with it. It is not to beat it because it is not doing what we want, not to starve it, not to burn it out, but to just look at it objectively and try to understand the language of life that our own body and system is using to express its needs. It needs to rest; it needs to be nourished; it needs to relax; it needs to be recognized as having value by everything else around it.

———————◆———————

Either we are taking the outer substance, the shell or the tension of the situation, or we are getting beneath it. It is really a question of mining from everyone and digging into everyone so that we do not allow the surface of the situation to become activated. If you are talking to the tensions of somebody, you stop relating. You are feeding your energy into tension, and the tension will grow. But if you can detach, what you are consciously doing is not allowing the personality and the tension to connect with you. You are denying that connection because you wish for a deeper connection.

It is like with my mother. She called today and she wanted instant service on something. I can see where she is wrong, and I can see where it is not right to bother people with the things she wants, but it is even more wrong to identify with the situation. The minute you identify with it, you are feeding it. You become one with the tension. But you can say, "Fine,

this is her tension, and I don't want to deal with that."
You do not do something negative just because you
see that she is wrong. So she is free. She comes in to
the store and she is happy. She has not done anything
deliberate. It is really the energy working through her,
testing me. If you respond to that tension, what happens? You keep somebody locked in and you yourself
are locked in with them. We become a prisoner with
everybody and we become free with nobody.

You only become free with somebody when
you dig beneath the tension, when you will not relate
to all the questions in your mind: "Maybe they meant
this, maybe they meant that, maybe they did this,
maybe they did that." You surrender that, and you
try to open and find out what the reality is. Try to dig
a little deeper and not go into the superficial tension.

You have to feel secure with people, you have
to love them, you have to want to love them, you have
to want to grow with them. Every action you do
should be an action that allows for the future. You are
putting your energy into something that will go up.
You are not allowing yourself to act like a beast, an animal, or to have all these crazy tensions. You surrender,
not because you are a nincompoop and you are trying
to be a sweet person, but because you can't afford to
get caught in the jaws of this tremendous tension.

———◆———

Growing is an emptying out and a filling up.
That way you begin to refine, purify, and in every

way nourish the muscles in the body and the chakras. With nourishment, every muscle, tissue, and organ in you begins to sprout and grow. And as you grow, it is essential to rid yourself of the congestion that forms. The very nature of growth is that you are refining your energy, and if you do not flush out the waste product, then the old pattern re-forms. You should practice the exercise of taking a deep breath in your heart and surrendering negative psychic tensions and congestion. If you do not flush out, this tension forms again and you can't change a pattern in your life. You really can't free yourself unless, as you refine your energy, you get rid of the unassimilated energies. So you slowly rise, and every time you work, you break up continually all your energy, and it separates just like churned milk. You keep the butter and you throw away the lesser product. The lesser product is really what we use, or what we should use, to live with. We work in our ordinary day, we have relationships, all of this is the by-product of life.

———◆———

Tension is very strong energy. It is very strong energy. You breathe deeply and draw the tension inside. It is just like chewing food. You suck the life energy out of the tension. What you can't suck out, you release a couple of times a day. You are eating food, digesting inside what you can of this food, and then you are getting rid of the by-products. The only way you can grow consciously is by eating the tensions of the day and then allowing what you can't eat to wash out. That way your life becomes compact and it becomes strong.

As you grow creatively, as you consciously assimilate the energy in the flow of your life force and you wash out the negative psychic tensions and congestion, you are creating a mechanism inside yourself. You are taking yourself from a little wigwam structure to a steel-reinforced high-rise inside. You are making a compressor and an extractor and you are building all kinds of machinery inside. You are putting wiring inside you, a sewer inside, a whole structure. Once you finish this structure then it demands another chemistry. This has to do with the capacity of the mechanism to refine any product and turn out something more capable. You are creating a generator, a generator which is opening you up, burning up your raw material. If you do not use raw material, what happens? You become impoverished. If you use it, then you can open more and more and more.

———◆———

Some of you will work a few months and then you will feel a band around your head. It is like a one-inch band of iron or steel. This means nothing except that you have removed some of your surface tension, the one-inch layer of shit, or whatever you wear as protection in the world. You have to be grateful that you feel this band. Most people live in the layer above that. They live in a world of illusion. People walk around saying, "Oh, I love everybody blah, blah, blah . . . ." Behind them there is a total disaster. They destroy everything they go near. They give bad advice to everyone they touch. Everything they do is terrible. They work for six months and they finally melt away this external mass, this external surface. Then they begin to understand that they are an uptight person. They feel this band around their heads.

This real band of tension that we live with usually takes six months to a year to break. We can't afford to realize what our condition actually is. It is so bad that we can't begin to realize it. Only after working in a positive way do we begin to see that we have a lock on our heart, a band of tension around our head, and what feels like a bar of steel on our shoulders. These things go away as we come out of this prison that we have built and will not admit exists.

So when you feel these things, what you are feeling is very real. You should be deeply grateful for it. This band of tension that you are coming to is a gift. It is an achievement. So feel it, but do not feed it. When you think about it you are feeding it. Just surrender it and you will dissolve it. That tension will dissolve and you will slowly absorb it inside in your growth. One day it will be gone.

In this life we are wrapped in a layer of tension meant to make us look like a Christmas package. It is like putting twenty or thirty years of shit in a lead container so you can't smell it, painting it with stars, sprinkling it with sparkles, putting a couple of cherries on it and saying, "What a great Christmas present." God help you when you break it open! As it begins to break open and we see all of this shit we think, "This is the reward for working?" Of course it is the reward for working. Do you want this stuff to eat into your kidneys, your heart, your mind, and every organ in your body? It has to stink as you begin to clean up this mess that you call you.

When I was with the Shankaracharya, I only asked him one question about growing. He said, "What do you want?" I said, "Well, I want to grow. I want to suffer and I want to grow."

He said, "That's not right. You should say you want to grow and you want to be happy." So I finally said, "Yes, I want to grow and I want to be happy." And he said, "You're going to suffer like a jackass for twenty-five more years." I started to laugh. I said, "Why?" He said, "Because of the way you were conceived. You were conceived in a tremendous hatred.

Your mother and father hated each other violently, so your soul was locked in great tension."

I really began to understand, then. And it is not their fault; it is nobody's fault. This is your karma. This is your ball game; you either play the game, break through it and clean it up, or you do not. It is not going to change. You accept it, you surrender it, and you become grateful that you can at least know what is wrong. It is our ignorance of our situation that makes us a prisoner. It is our ability to grow inside that breaks these bonds and frees us.

Nobody did it to you. The wheel was spun and it landed on number 6002XYZ. Out you came and you got this situation. But within you there is also the ability to cope with it. The shit and poison that you were born through, those tensions and those problems that you were born through, are the exact chemical components to make the particular fertilizer that nourishes the kind of plant that you are. This is the perfection of our life. If you took all of the quantities — all of the negatives and all of the positives — and you ground it down and put one teaspoon of that in a glass of water and drank it, you would be a free human being. All of this stuff that you call your karma is exactly what you need to grow free.

———◆———

Your struggle, this struggle within you, is only to eat energy, feed muscles, and deal with the tensions and the pain that these muscles feel as they open. It is simple. We have a very simple work. The problem is that energy manifests. Because of this we imagine a lot, we visualize a lot, we sense a lot. But the *less* we sense, the less mind we use, the less emotions we use, the more capable we become of taking in energy and allowing ourselves to accept our growth simply. The tensions that we make and the limitations that we put upon ourselves are the problem, because there really is no limitation. Finally, as you grow more, you can take in the pains that come as these muscles and bones expand in you. These pains only represent growth. You can drink them in and simultaneously keep your heart open. You can take in this pain as energy with gratitude. Then you have a chance to make a great leap. This leap will allow you to take in faster, burn faster, and give off more.

But if you can't surrender, if you can't work properly, you must see that this limitation is only a stubbornness and a resistance in you. You have to really fight yourself. You are letting something gain control of you because you are lazy or stupid. It is as simple as that. There is no excuse for ignorance, because by doing, working, just taking a breath, you are eating through the tensions that keep you from making this effort. The only thing that exists for you in the world is doing this for a half hour once or twice a day, and trying in your ordinary relationships with people to internalize the situation; not to identify, not to talk and talk, but to drink in and feel the flow of life between you and another human being.

Then you are using your energy in a positive and simple way, and you are not getting tense and tight and excited.

————◆————

The need to think of oneself as pure is ego. If you had any idea of the thickness, the molecular density, of a human being compared to the infinite energy that flows through the atmosphere, it would frighten you to the point where it would become impossible for you to work. But we live in a state of grace. God is an extraordinarily generous and good energy that allows us to live in an atmosphere that is just barely possible for us. Beyond that, It allows us to move to the next level. We are structured in such a way that we always have the ability to rise to level after level. It is an infinite amount of work that is supported by an infinite grace. Life is structured so that only when you get to one level can you visualize the next. From there you go on and on and on. It is the ability to live this way that allows you to expand and love everything and everybody, to include the entire universe within yourself.

The Wish to Grow

*My wish is to grow,
my wish is only to grow, and whatever else
happens can happen.*

T here is no charity in spiritual work. It has to do solely with opening to receive. If you do not open to receive, you absolutely will not get it. So please try to find inside yourself a deep thing that wants. I have, after thirty-eight years, a deep burning inside my heart that wants tremendously. It has always wanted tremendously. Until the day I die, I will want tremendously. And if I do not feel that hunger, then I work until I feel my heart open very, very deeply. My wish is to grow, my wish is only to grow, and whatever else happens can happen, but that is strictly the by-product of this wish inside me to grow more conscious and to become more enlightened.

———◆———

You have to have, inside yourself, an appetite. You have to really want. Unfortunately, spiritual attainments have nothing to do with time, they have to do with intent. If there is a depth in you that really wants and you open from this depth, you can do everything.

A superficial person working extraordinarily hard will get a superficial result fast, but somebody working from depth will get everything. This wish that goes in, in, in, that opens from the core, makes it possible.

———————◆———————

You have to feel inside, before you even do your exercise, that you have asked and asked and asked deeply within yourself. You do this on your way to class. You do not sit down and say, "Well, here we are, it's another Thursday night, we'll get together and I'll do a little of my work. Okay, let's open." This will never happen. If you can't thaw out a lamb chop in a half hour, you certainly can't thaw out your inner being. Unless you really ask during the day, and keep asking, you can't get to a new depth. You can't come to class and begin your exercise; your exercise should be part of your day.

———————◆———————

Your will can attract everything you need. If you do not have what you want, if you find you are not getting the satisfaction you want, then you have to look in the mirror and say, "Stupid!" Because you are being very, very stupid.

It is all within us. Every human being is born with a capacity to have everything that exists in this world. If it does not happen, it is because you are lazy and sloppy, and you do not even have this concept in your head. I am giving it to you to put in your head. You have to keep it there, and you have to want to be happy, free, and completely realized. There is nothing else. It has to be there, and every time something goes wrong you have to look in the mirror and say, "All right, jerk, what did you do?"

What did *you* do? Not this person or that person or somebody else. What did *you* do? Or what are you *not* doing now? Are you open, are you breathing, is your energy in flow, are you conscious of what you want or what your objective is?

It is ridiculous when people come, whining and crying, saying, "Oh, Rudi, oh, Rudi." It is unbelievable! It represents unconsciousness. They are saying, "I have forgotten what I was born for and what I can do." This is all they are expressing.

For myself, I am never going to have anything but an absolutely wonderful life. Nobody and nothing is going to give me less than that, because I really want to meet God. And when I meet Him, I do not want to be in a wheelchair, bandaged up, with one leg off, and my nose cut, and my eyes blind and so on. I want to go there laughing, singing, and having one hell of a good time. I really want to enjoy my life. I do not have to walk around covered with a hair shirt, with chains around my ankles, crying and beating myself with a lash to prove that I love God.

God can't be loved that way; that is an expression of self-hatred. You can love God by loving yourself and loving God and really working your way up. It starts with how you express your energy. You accept the fact that you can transcend every second and that every negative thing that happens to you is an expression of your limitation, your stupidity, and your absolute laziness. The combination of laziness and stupidity is all that stops you from being realized.

———————◆———————

To sit complacently, not wishing, not wanting, not burning inside — this is the limitation. The only thing that does not burn is a wet mattress or wet newspapers. You have to open inside, really bring this wish in you. It is the most heartbreaking thing of all for me to see so many of you who do not have enough depth, who do not want, who do not ask and open. I have so much energy; I have so much to give you. But it is just like watching trucks backing up to the Hudson and pouring out millions of gallons of milk. My energy goes out into the atmosphere because there are not enough people among all of you who want what I have. So I work and I grow because I keep going around and around in myself. But I really need communication; I need people who want to ask, who want to take, and who want to grow. It is your wish — it is your mind and your heart wanting so much — that qualifies you.

So you sit here, you drink into yourself, you feel your muscles taking in this energy in a hungry way and growing inside, and you feel yourself open. If you can't make yourself hungry, then you sit at night and you ask and ask and ask. In the Bible it says repeatedly, "Ask and ye shall receive." You have to ask endlessly. You can ask for four hours, you can ask fifty thousand times, until you find in you such a wish to grow, such a wanting to grow, such an openness, that your hunger allows you to take in a thousand times more. There is no limit to the capacity of a person to take in and grow.

———◆———

I have said it at least five thousand times, and I will say it five thousand and one times: if you want to grow, then you sit in meditation, you bring your mind inside, and you ask. It should be the same way you would ask if you had a child who was dying. You would pray and you would ask God. The emotion would open your heart, and you would ask, even if you claim you do not believe in such a thing. You have to ask and ask inside. And you keep asking and asking. Hear yourself say inside, "I want to grow." Keep repeating that. First it sounds superficial, then emotional, and then you feel your heart really open. You have asked so much that you are bringing energy into the heart chakra. Then you keep asking and asking and asking, and the nourishment inside suddenly expands, and your heart opens. Then you have a place to grow from. You have really opened your heart to your wish.

You bring your mind there and you say inside, "I want to grow," and you keep saying this out loud until you hear the tone change in your voice, until you feel the emotion change in your voice, and then you keep saying it until you feel your heart break open. Keep asking and asking and asking until you feel the emotion drilling into your heart. Then you will feel this wish going in deeper and deeper. Keep drilling as long as you can. Breathe in your heart and let this wish pierce it. It cracks it open just as if you were breaking open a coconut.

A wish in a human being is extraordinary. It is so fine that it can soak through anything. It can go through bone; it can go through skin; it can go through steel. It penetrates like a laser beam. You keep wishing and wishing and wishing, and you cut right through into the deepest part of you.

But you can't understand until you do it. How can you understand unless you do it?

———◆———

There is an aspect of our growth that in many ways makes it difficult for people to sustain an even pace of growing. This is resistance. Resistance is very much like the water mechanism on a furnace: it comes up by demand. Because of the many conflicting elements in the murky depths of the unconscious, we develop resistance to cut off the supply of nourishment that we take within ourselves.

Resistance, or the inability to take love or energy, or to grow, is unconsciously allowing ourselves to grow at a rate that *we* will. In other words, we are not surrendering to God, we are not surrendering to Creative Energy, we are governed by our own will. This is extraordinarily deeply ingrained in many people.

Growing is a question of assimilating energy, consciously allowing this flow to come down. When the resistance comes, you have to look at it objectively as if it were in somebody else. You begin to understand that it is just a mechanism of your own mind that allows you to stop and say, "I don't wish to take in any more, I will close off, I will block off inside." This bolt goes "Clink," and finally your mechanism closes. Your eyes go dead. Inside you feel that everyone is imposing themselves on you. It is their will against your will, they are forcing you, and it goes on and on. It is thousands of justifications; it is unreal and unconscious.

———◆———

Often we study with someone not because we want to learn and change, but because it justifies our staying the way we are. Resistance takes place in the marriage between two people, and it certainly takes place in the marriage of energies between a student and a teacher.

Growth always manifests itself through resistance. It is the same thing in a marriage: you learn as the resistance starts moving around and the passion wears down. Then consciousness is needed to take the place of passion.

———————◆———————

You have to feel inside yourself that you are drinking in a force. You have to feel the force expand in you, feel that your muscles and tissues are expanding and growing, and feel the energy coming up your spinal column. If you do not feel that, you are not being nourished and no growth can possibly be taking place. On a physical level, all you do is get a headache. On a spiritual level, you get another type of headache because you can actually feel the expansion. Like yeast or bacteria expanding, a life force expands in you. You have every sense of it being more than yourself because it creates one thing — resistance. Unless you feel resistance inside, no real growth is taking place.

Complacency and insanity have to do with energy that is not harnessed, energy that appears out there, brilliant ideas that are ungrounded because there is no energy connection to them. Consciousness and conscious growth involve an evolving dynamic force that raises itself every day just a fraction, so that it is a vital thing. It is like a stem and a flower. It has a root system. You feel the energy coming down, you feel your heart expanding, you feel it through your chest, you feel your chakras, you feel it going through your sex organ and up your spinal column.

That is the refinement of physical energy and its transference into spiritual force, so that it flows up and uplifts you. It is a higher force. It has absolutely nothing to do with you as a physical person; it has to do with you as a spiritual person being nourished through your own conscious effort, overcoming resistance and growing. The resistance can manifest when you lie down at night wishing you had died that day, because the pain of the expansion of these muscles is, at times, extraordinarily difficult. These muscles are locked and tight like a paralyzed hand. These are muscles that are not used. They are the conscious spiritual muscle system that can only be fed minutely, a little bit at a time.

The effort you have to make to have this flow take place in you is tremendous. Everything in you wants to run away. Everything in you wants to hide, but the only thing that can ever free you is to work and consciously breathe in and feel the secretion of the energy in your body as you work and gather it in. This energy is a higher energy. It is only gathered with tremendous resistance. That is why very few people who exist on the earth ever have within them such a structure. When you meet such a person, you see it in the bone structure of his or her head. You see it in his or her every muscle.

The thing you must understand, however, is that conscious work is in the act of transcending. This means you are always working consciously and overcoming resistance. It is the only way you can differentiate between an illusion and reality. An illusion is something that goes by itself, and conscious work has to do with stretching and overcoming resistance in yourself.

———◆———

I have endlessly seen students reach a certain point where, if they stayed for the next two months, they would change. But, they always pick just that time to go away — they have to go on a vacation, this is their time to go away. They know inside what they are doing. It is the inability to be consistent in taking nourishment.

Consistency in your nourishment, consistency in what you take in, in your meditation and in your exercise, is your guarantee to growth. So when you feel things beginning to close inside, they are not closing, exactly — they are calling for more effort. Suddenly you have hit a different stratum and you have to connect on a higher level. You have to make more of an effort to get the same amount of energy to keep this process going.

When we hit these points we say, "Well, this is not a good time to work, obviously there is this resistance in me, and I'm going to slow it down." And what happens? You abort your entire effort. You have dug halfway through the mountain, and then you turn around and come back out of the mountain and say, "Oh, I've come out into the sunshine." You have not come out into the sunshine. You have blown your energy on a great effort, and you have gotten absolutely no reward for it whatsoever, because you have always backed off from the moment of conscious additional effort.

Spirituality is based on the consistent flow of energy in you from a higher place. Your not breaking down, your not finding how to make your connection to keep this consistency going, has to do with the lack of conscious effort in you. If a mother does not drink milk, the child inside her is going to draw calcium out of her fingernails if it needs to. The child can take it out of her bones. In spirituality, you have to make the effort. When you find the pressure is on, then sit down and work your guts out.

You are going to be exhausted at the end of the day anyway. It is better to be exhausted working consciously so you will rip out of this insane period like a miner stealing gold out of a mountain. You are taking a treasure out of a situation that would otherwise leave you with nothing but garbage. There are certain times when it does not matter what you do, you are going to be absolutely torn apart. There are days when nothing is going to go right, so then you fight like a jackass to take out what you need for your exercise. Only that kind of effort will consistently give you a spiritual life. Only that kind of effort.

When something becomes a reason not to find nourishment, not to dig for it, then you are not a spiritual person. You are an ordinary person being affected on the physical level. A spiritual person takes it up and digs out. Nothing and no reason in the world could stop you from finding the nourishment that you need to feed yourself inside. If it is hard for you, it does not matter. You need thirty minutes a day of conscious effort to feed yourself. If you can't do that, then you work five minutes every hour. You tear yourself apart. You can certainly get five minutes an hour for six hours; there is no excuse not to.

The harder it is for you to find that energy, the harder it is for you to surrender, the closer you are to the end of a tunnel. Dramatic things always take place then. It is like putting out seeds in the garden — every crow is going to come. What you have is an investment of energy lying out there like birdseed on a balcony. It does not become yours until you break through the last inch of that tunnel. Then the energy comes back in you. Nature will never let you have that until you fight your guts out and finish it.

You have to realize that you only get this energy inside you through your own effort. When spirituality is described in terms of a person climbing a mountain, going through a forest and all that, it is a metaphor for the person who has the guts not to accept a "no." The person will go through everything; he or she will crawl, will drag along, will do anything else, but will not accept a "no." And the person gets the day's energy. You have to learn that. You have to fight for this energy inside, for this nourishment inside. It does not matter what the situation is. It does not matter whether you are getting married or being buried, if you forget to work that day, you can forget about your life. You have lost your link between yourself and God.

Detachment

Being detached has nothing to do with not having; it has to do with not holding.

S ome people go into a religious or philosophical teaching and find that it separates them from their friends, from their family, and from all their ordinary attachments. This is a common occurrence with people who join spiritual groups. They become fanatical, and irrationally so. Instead of expanding the love they feel for their friends and neighbors, they begin to consider themselves superior. Everyone else is inferior. They know they are enlightened, they have all the answers, and everyone else is an enemy. That certainly does not express what spirituality is supposed to be. It should expand us. It should incorporate everyone, eventually, in the flow and harmony of our existence. And it certainly should not set up negative quantities and make enemies of the people we were friendly with before.

I have seen this within families where a young person, or even an older person, gets bitten by some teaching. They endlessly proselytize. They grind out this thing that has just been poured into them without any digestion. They will give off a speech for three or four hours, like a mass propaganda machine. There is no chance for them to really come to their own minds. They have been structured as if cement was poured into them. They go on and on and on. You do not feel depth with them, you do not feel love, and you certainly do not feel communication.

The idea of growing spiritually is that you should consciously nourish everybody that you come into contact with. It is not meant to separate you from people, but to open you to other people.

———◆———

It is essential for people who are trying to do spiritual work to return to their roots. The roots in this case are what they come from — their own background, race, religion, and culture. It is the expression of very uptight people to attack their country, to attack their parents, to attack their culture. It is really an attack on themselves. They are turning on themselves and expressing their self-hatred.

How can we hate what we come from and ever have a sense of enlightenment? We have to unfold the tensions of our root system to nourish what we come from and allow it to unfold, to reveal itself. Then you understand that God, or Creative Energy, or whatever you care to call it, is perfect. It has given you the most positive — and the only — way for you to evolve as an individual.

We have to recognize our individual creativity and potential. We do not try to emulate somebody else, but we try to work within ourselves to have our energy grow, accumulate, nourish us inside, and continually break down our tensions.

———◆———

The energy should nourish you enough to make the people next to you grow. It should not separate you from the people immediately next to you. If it separates you from them, then it is an illusion. An illusion is when your ego feels tremendously good, but the effect is to separate you from the people around you. An illusion is ego without any content.

Anything that makes you grow has content. That content not only should nourish you, but it should also feed the immediate area around you. So often when people do spiritual work it completely alienates them from their friends and family. They get clumped together with a group of people who are into the same thing, and they all tell each other how wonderful they are. That is not a real appraisal of the situation. A real appraisal comes from your own children, your father and mother, your sisters and brothers, those of your own blood. Then you go to outside people.

When something closes you away from the people next to you, then you are in a very deep illusion, because the thing that you think you have is taking you away from your own root system. Your root system is that which eventually will connect you with God, because God gave you that. It is real, not artificial.

There is no sense in trying to build castles in the air. You have to put in a basement, you have to put in a furnace, you have to put in a sewer, you have to put in toilets, you have to put in heating, you have to put in water, you have to have a bar of soap. Spirituality has to provide those things. It does not give the promise of a castle in the air. It gives you everything, including garbage pickup. You have to understand that. You can't grow and be putting your energy in little sacks and tying it and laying it on the side, storing it up. This is the thing that will destroy you.

The very nature of growing spiritually is that the by-product of the tension that is broken down is completely cleared away at the end of the day. It is a removal system. It breaks down tensions, it breaks down animosity, it breaks down prejudice, and it brings, slowly, love and freedom and realization.

And nobody can be realized who is not in the immediate vicinity of his or her own family, and background, and everything else. If you can't accept yourself, inside your own heart, then of course your heart does not open, because you are protecting yourself from the people whom you have come from, the people who have supported you, who have gotten you that far.

Not only do you have to love, you have to love deeply and rationally. To love a bum on the street while you will not give your grandmother a cup of coffee — this is not love. It is a coward's way of projecting a momentary commitment instead of a deep commitment, which has to do with what you come from and where you live.

It is like people talking ecology and dropping garbage out the window. And believe me, most of the people who talk ecology do drop garbage out the window because they are busy on the outside and not really concerned with the inside.

Everything has to be an internal condition. Those closest to you — your parents, your wife, your children, and the people who you came up with — represent that manifestation. Anyone can put some money down on a bar and get a lot of people to drink beer. That is a very easy thing to do. Turning on people over there while you are not turning on the people next to you has to do with, again, the same kind of illusion.

Reality is being responsible from the inside out, and more than anything else, finding out and being conscious of what stops your heart from opening, what stops your own inner functioning. The attachments of the people closest to you give you your energy. Anyone who tries to separate you from that is trying to give you an illusion. If you separate people from their energy, or their energy contacts, then you can control them. They will respond very easily to anything that is given.

Reality is being deeply responsible. It is working, it is holding a job, it is supporting the people who you are responsible to. It is not going from place to place, fathering children; it is taking care of the child that you fathered. Yet so many people run around in this promiscuous way.

The work we are doing is meant to get you the energy within yourself to support you and the area around you. When you do that successfully then the energy will rise in you because you have your foundation inside. It is a very real and a very practical thing.

———◆———

Working with higher forces is only possible when we, in our ordinary life, have dealt with our attachments properly, on a mature level. This is illustrated by the tree of life. The higher the tree rises, the more the roots go out, and the more is drawn from the external world into the internal system of the tree. A human being also grows from his attachments expanding him, and from the externalized energy, which is slowly drawn into him. He is slowly detaching himself from the physical level of the earth, because of his increased consciousness.

To take an ax and chop yourself free from all these things does not represent maturity — it represents nothing more than stupidity. When you reject your heritage, your religion, your race, everything that you come from, you have stopped taking in within you that energy that you come from. This is your root system. You absolutely cannot grow without having these roots. You also do not fulfill your karma. It is very difficult to grow with your mother and father on one side, your hang-ups on the other side, and your sense of guilt on another, but this is what growing is about. It means staying attached and transcending every one of these things.

Slowly the tree goes up a little bit, up a little bit, and the roots go deeper. Then you begin to draw in, from your parents, from your religion, from your race, from your culture, the energy that you need to grow.

The only thing people can do who have detached from their roots is create illusions. Without roots, without that which goes deeply into the earth and holds you, without that which comes from discipline and responsibility, you become more and more of an illusionist. The people who run from ashram to ashram and teacher to teacher become freaked out. This one told them that, and that one told them this, and their system inside goes crazy, because you can't draw energy from a multitude of places. You can draw from one place; if you are not successful there, you draw from two. But you can't run and draw here and draw there, except in the most superficial way.

In every sense, commitment and longevity allow for spirituality. You have grown and transcended. You can do this with me; you can do it with anybody. If I do not work for you, fine, go someplace else, but you have to stay there, you have to mature and grow in the soil of whatever situation it is. And whatever is real or unreal or right or wrong in the situation is secondary to whether or not you get energy and whether or not you are growing. It is the growing that makes you free because you are drawing in energy. You are drawing in a force on this level and possibly on a higher level. You can only tell that you are drawing it on a higher spiritual level if you find you are detaching yourself from all the situations that exist on the earth level. Are you more mature in your attitude with your friends and your parents? Are you more mature in your attitude with yourself? Do you have a schedule of sleeping and eating properly? Do you have a sense of belonging?

People who do not feel they belong are people who do not draw energy into themselves. We are not born as air plants, things suspended in space. We have to be planted firmly in the earth to take this higher energy that is found in space. It is a matter of discipline, responsibility, knowledge, and all these other things that exist on an earth level, raised to a higher energy level. You can only reach to the highest spiritual levels with the highest and finest force within yourself.

———◆———

There is a difference between being detached and not having. You can have. I have. I do not care whether everything I have goes underground. This does not bother me, but it does not mean that I will not be responsible.

There is a big difference between being attached and detached. You can be attached and have a penny in your pocket, and you can be detached and have a million dollars. People always think that detachment has to do with not having. Being detached has nothing to do with not having; it has to do with not *holding*. There are people who love and are not possessive, and there are people who do not love and *are* possessive.

In our life, the expression of detachment can only manifest when you are attached to something that transcends everything on the earth level. This translates into our attachment for spiritual growth. We can have and be detached if our attachment is to that which is beyond ourselves, if it transcends the level of the earth.

━━━◆━━━

I had an experience about two months ago when a girl whom I know very well came into my store. She was being very generous, and she said, "If you could have a wish, what would you wish for?" I said, "It doesn't really matter," because the question is rather ridiculous. Then I said, "Well, if you really want to know, I would wish that a fire appeared. And if a fire appeared and I could step into it and be burned alive and this would not change anybody's karma who I would ever know, I would be very happy to step into that fire."

This is really the truth for me. I have not had, since I was about one day old, any sense of attachment to earth, because on the day I was born, I was dropped down a flight of stairs and everything in me was ripped. I was ripped continually until I was about fourteen, and by that time I had five hundred other things ripping me. I have been ripped and ripped and ripped in this life.

When I was ten and a half, I made a vow of detachment. I have had everything that I ever was attached to taken away from me over and over and over again. At this point in my life I am deeply grateful for that, because you never have within yourself the capacity to function for anyone else, or yourself, in an attached state.

The most terrifying thing is when you really love somebody. To be emotionally attached to a person gives you the one condition that is detrimental to the relationship — a lack of objectivity. You never can really and truly give advice to a person you love and are attached to. It is a strange, ironic side of life, because all that we do, all that we try for as people, is to secure the people whom we love. The more we try to secure them and the more attached we become to them, the less able we are to do a proper job.

This is the only reason to work, because if you truly love people then you have to have a spiritual life to function for them. You have to be detached from them. You can always tell someone's spirituality by that person's ability to free you at the cost to themselves. Not to bind you, because when people try to bind you to them, it expresses their need to be attached to you. When they can free you, it represents their love for you, because their detachment will allow you to grow.

When somebody tells you they have you next to them for your sake, then you had better watch out, because nobody in this world is ever able to be helped unless there is a detached situation. When somebody says they are doing something for your sake, it is like the song in *Man of La Mancha*, "I'm only thinking of him . . . ," and this goes on and on and on as the refrain. Everyone is taking from everyone else, and then always saying how good it is for the other person.

If you have any sense of value for people, and you want to live and you want to love, then you have to grow. In our society, the whole understanding of love is completely off. I have seen so many people, older couples — the man dies, and then the woman dies. They call this a great love. It is not a great love, it is a great attachment. And it is proof of one thing: the relationship did not have enough nourishment to feed two people. It was just barely enough to sustain one. So when one died, the other died also. This is not a real situation. If a relationship really has content, if it really has nourishment, then it should be able to feed not only two, it should also be able to feed any offspring that come from it. But in our culture, we think of love as that which compels us to die for another human being. Love is that which fulfills us in our attachment on this physical level, so that we are free and detached to have a spiritual life.

It is very hard to explain this particular thing to people, because it takes tremendous energy inside, it takes growing inside you, to fulfill yourself to the point of being detached from somebody whom you love. It is very real and very light. So if that person says, "Look, I want to go here," you say, "Fine, you need that, then you go."

———————————

We have to learn that our reason for living on a physical level is to fulfill the energy quantity of the physical level and become detached from it. You can't be detached from money until you have money; you can't be detached from love, physical love, until you have had physical love. Nobody can give away that which they do not have. If you really want to grow spiritually and become mature, you have to try to be highly conscious, to grow inside, by saving as much energy as possible and growing away from everything on the physical level.

I find amazing the advice that is so often given in spiritual work. People at a tender age, when they are very inexperienced, are told, "No, you can't do this, you can't do that, you can't do this, you can't do that." Never, then, can they learn detachment, because the maturity from which detachment can come has not been allowed to develop in them. Of course, it is not right to have certain situations; it certainly is not right to waste sexual energy. But how in the world can you be free of sexual attachments until you have experienced what sexual energy costs you in your spiritual life? *You* have to transcend it; *you* have to make the choice. If it is not your choice, if it is not done through your own will and your own consciousness, then you will come back the next life and have to work it out again.

Every situation, every change you make, has to come from within you and your own consciousness. Not from somebody else's consciousness, but from your consciousness. If you wish to limit yourself to speed your maturity, that is intelligent. In the same way, if you want to work harder and earn more money to free yourself from worries about money, that also makes sense. Maturity has to do with how you spend your money, how you spend your time, and what you do with both of these things. They free you.

Once when I was in my twenties, somebody called me and said a certain teacher was in town, somebody whom I was very anxious to hear speak. I was able to hail a taxi, jump in, and run uptown. At that point, two dollars and fifty cents was remarkable and wonderful. If I had had to take the subway, I would have missed the opportunity. Money allows us to do. This is what money is for. But it also represents consciousness. Money is not obtainable without consciousness. It is the consciousness you use in your life that frees you to be able to do these things.

———◆———

Celibate or not celibate, it does not matter. It does not matter at all unless you are using that energy. If you do not have a very deep, vital inner life and you have not harnessed your energy and used it to transcend the physical situation, it does not matter what you do with your energy. It does not matter if you pee in the stream if you are not going to drink from it. What does it matter? If it is not going to be used for a real reason, it does not matter what you do with it.

What does it matter if people are celibate if they never use that energy for their growth? What are they being celibate for? For an illusion. Sexual energy is very strong, very vital energy. But it has no meaning whatsoever unless it is harnessed and used properly. So what is there to not do? Celibacy for the sake of celibacy is like taking your food every day and throwing it in the compost heap. If it is not feeding somebody else, and it is not feeding you, and you are not using it spiritually, then it does not make any difference. Sexuality comes from an energy that has to be used with consciousness, otherwise it does not matter what your reasons are for not doing it.

Either there is a conscious effort, which produces a conscious result that carries you toward your enlightenment, or it is another kind of illusion. You can put somebody down and feel superior — you are a little virgin with a little frozen smile on your face. Big deal. You will never have enlightenment that way. These things have no meaning. It is a very practical thing. The energy has to be used properly. And, you do not use your spiritual life to bludgeon somebody else.

I get students who are tired of having a sexual relationship with their husband or wife, so they stop immediately, because they have decided it is anti-spiritual.

They did not enjoy it; they never functioned right. But spirituality becomes their excuse; they suddenly are spiritual, so they can't screw. This is not consciousness. It is not a way of transcending. It is a way of lying. It is a way of cheating. And there is no sacrifice in it. You are sacrificing somebody else, not yourself.

Never give away anything you do not really want. Work your way out of it. You have to use that energy; you transcend it. You transcend it with resistance.

I had a very nice kid come to see me who teaches another form of meditation — physical, rather like aikido. He came and said, very proudly, that he had been celibate for two years. I looked at him and said, "You know, I like you, and I've known you for about a year and a half. Tell me, how active were you before?" He looked at me, and he said, "Not very." I said, "So what did you do?"

It is a convenience. Not that he should or should not be celibate, but why make a lie out of it? You say to yourself, "Fine, I am cold and I really don't have this capacity to give." Then at least you are honest. But do not pretend you are making a sacrifice. Renunciation has to do with renouncing what you want, not what you do not want. Everyone can give up spinach. You have to give up what you really want in this life. That is what a sacrifice is about. You do not sacrifice a dead cat or a dead dog or a dead passion. You sacrifice living things. And you try to revive dead ones, so then later you can sacrifice them. It is much better to bring the fire to life and then put it out with consciousness than to sit over a dead fire and pretend you are having a *puja*.

You have to have something to give it away. You have to want something to sacrifice it. This is one of the biggest obstacles for people who claim spirituality. They do not work because they think working is dirty. It becomes a cop-out. Growing has to do with consciously transcending yourself and making sacrifices — not things that you wish to sacrifice, but things that your consciousness demands you sacrifice.

———◆———

You have to *have* before you can surrender. A lot of people talk about surrender when they have nothing to surrender. You have to work yourself into a situation, transcend it, and then you can surrender it. It is easy to say, "Money is shit." Have money and give it away, and then see how detached you are from it. Do a job so brilliantly that you free yourself from it. Do anything wonderfully well. Not doing is not an expression of freedom. It is the expression of being a sloth. It is without muscle. It has only to do with illusion. You have to understand the difference between doing and illusion.

———————◆—————

Every act that you do during your day should be done from the premise of detachment. You have to consciously detach yourself so that you can be above the situation, and then you are freer. You are not completely free, but you are freer to see the situation because of the flow of energy that exists there. By pulling away and slowly rising, you create a vacuum through which this energy can flow. This is the basic principle of growth.

Any attachment we have does not allow for growth. You consciously have to detach continually even from the people whom you love or with whom you feel secure, to continue growing. The greatest symbol of this is a mother feeding a child from her breast. She has to take the child off and belch it so that the milk is assimilated properly in the child. We, in growing, have to be detached, sometimes for longer or shorter periods, so that we can absorb the energy and the creative juice trying to raise itself in us. Too much attachment is very bad because it degenerates the chemistry. This is something we have to be aware of. Some people are more in need than others, but there still has to be a separation, a detachment, otherwise a very weak and infirm situation develops.

.

Surrender

If you are not strong enough to trust, you will destroy your connection to Creative Energy. It is the simplest thing in the world. It is the flowing of life without our involvement in any way, shape, or form.

I t takes a tremendous letting go to stop these hands, these emotions, and this mind, all of which want to touch and handle the energy that comes through us. Every one of our senses that touches this spiritual energy diminishes it enormously.

Human life can only be created when a couple comes together and the semen goes into the woman without touching the atmosphere at all. If you tried to observe the process there would be no child, because of the impurity of our atmosphere.

In the same way, only when we can surrender in ourselves and not let this flow of energy through ourselves be tainted by any one of our senses do we have a chance. We can't ever know about it. Either it comes from God or it does not come from God. One has to, finally, drop the question. The more you handle it, the more you touch it, the more you think about it, the less capability it has to free you. All you have to do is try to open and let this force come in untainted. Just be responsible for bringing it through the chakras, through the sex organs and up the spine. You do not have to know. You are freed from that responsibility. You are freed from the bullshit of knowing.

If you are not strong enough to trust the process, you will destroy your connection to Creative Energy. It is the simplest thing in the world. It is the flowing of life without our involvement in any way, shape, or form. It has to do with letting the nothingness that is creativity flow through our system. Eventually it will dissolve even that system, and we will be free. Meanwhile, as we go through our life, we become free from so many other things because the sheer nutritional value of this force entering us and going through us is so much greater when we leave it alone.

It is not the amount you work, it is the depth you open, the amount you are willing to surrender, and the lack of reservation you have as far as what you are willing to give up that matters. Ultimately the process of growth has nothing to do with you at all. Your attitude — who you think you are or what you think you will do — has absolutely no meaning. Through your opening and deeply surrendering, *it* will take place.

This inner state of being will begin to function when you open to it, because it is an organic and natural thing, very much like a pineapple getting ripe on the tree. You open yourself to these higher levels of consciousness and energy. By receiving this energy, first all your organs, all your chakras and muscles, become complete. Then the energy flows in them and you become ripe. As you become ripe, you have extraordinary realizations. They are the realizations that take place in a ripe human being, like the sweetness that develops in a ripe pineapple.

It does not matter what you did in your life or what you are doing in your life. Spiritual growth has nothing to do with that, because the external things are simply momentary conditions. By taking in this more mature, deeply sweet, and nourishing energy and growing, things will change in you. It is living with the energy that allows you to change. It is a gift.

People *work* on their spiritual life. They consider where *they* are and where *it* is, and this goes on and on. But there is one thing you have to understand: all of this maneuvering is meaningless in itself. The real question is whether the energy connects for you in your spiritual exercise. You allow the force to work you, instead of you working the force. This energy, by its very nature, has to be the expression of God's will. It has nothing to do with your will.

We continually move around within ourselves trying to put ourselves in a better position. But that is like cutting down the gap between us and our goal by fifty percent every day. If you are a thousand miles away and tomorrow you are five hundred miles away, and so on, you will never get there. If you continually cut the distance in half, you will be dividing infinitesimally smaller and smaller things, but the gap will never disappear. It will become a membrane of your will and your personality that separates you from this spiritual force. Allow *it* to work *you* from its own will.

It is a very essential difference. It is like the case of being married to somebody where you do as much as you think the marriage demands. You do your half or your third or your eighty percent. That is the wrong approach, because a marriage means serving somebody else as he or she needs to be served.

It is exactly the same thing in a spiritual life. You do not appease this spiritual force, or God. You do not change as you see fit; you change as it is wanted. The only way to find out how it is wanted is to completely surrender, from within yourself, everything you feel or think — good, bad, or anything else.

Spirituality has to do with allowing this higher will to work in you. When you finally come to that point of surrender, then *it* will change things in you. It will change your chemistry; it will change all the physical manifestations. You will know it is working by the difference in your life. Instead of working spiritually, you will be spiritually worked.

This is basically what our work is about: you allow this energy to enter you. You will feel things working on you in your sleep. It is not anything you might welcome, but something you have to surrender to. All these energies we are surrendering to and allowing to work in us are just trying to take away the thicknesses, the different levels, the calluses we have accumulated over the endless time we have spent upon this world and in this atmosphere.

Spiritual work has to do with spirit and energy. As you free yourself and the energy comes out of you, it rises and rises and rises. Every time it rises further, it connects with another level of energy. That is how your freedom takes place. You attract from your being. As you rise to another dimension, the content of that pours into you. This is only possible by working, and working tremendously hard, because to take in new energy you have to have made muscles that can hold that energy. So our whole effort in life, as we grow, is to support with muscle, which is the result of work, the energy that increasingly comes within us.

————◆————

In your spiritual exercise you are getting fuel that can free you. The freeing of you is accomplished by your surrender. When you surrender, you open, and this vastness inside you opens. All these psychic muscles open and become nothing more than a great pipe through which this force works.

As the force works through you, you can begin to understand the relation of that flow of energy to Creation. It *is* Creation. When you begin to touch Creation and see life come through you and touch other people, you understand that you in no way have any right to think of it as yourself, no more than any parent has the right to feel that a child is theirs. It is their responsibility, it is not their creation. Just like a woman who is pregnant, you are a vehicle in which something can grow and through which something can flow.

The whole expression on the physical level is of our capacity to possess and to control. It is an instinct, a very simple instinct. The ability to love is to free everything you touch — not to limit it, not to make it less in any way. In your work every day you have one thing to do. That is to open, grow, expand more, to feel — *actually*, not symbolically — these muscles stretching, and increase the volume of energy that comes through you.

If you do not grow every day then you begin to have illusions about what you are doing. Then every time you attain something you want to think of it as yours. You are not working, you are not encompassing the energy that is there and the energy that was there. You are sitting back and taking credit for what happened yesterday.

You have to be very highly conscious, and you have to work tremendously deeply, to be able to transcend what was. Once you transcend a situation, you in no way have to justify what was. You have bettered the situation. Instead of carrying around inside you this enormous bookkeeping system, trying to figure out how much somebody owes you and how much you did for someone else, you absolutely have no need for any of it. You are continually on a higher level. You have worked above yourself and the energy has increased. It is completely capable of taking care of everything. It takes care of it; you have no need to take care of anything.

———◆———

Do you want to become an authority on you? What are you? You are congested, rusty pipes. Until you cut these out and replace them, nothing can take place in you. You are congested and filled with garbage, and you are trying to analyze the garbage and write books on it. You can't do that. You *can* do one thing: you can surrender *you* inside yourself — you can surrender your attachment to all the outside stuff, and use that energy internally to grow and transcend yourself. The day comes, finally, when you feel this flow of your life force expanding in you. The bump on your head is expanded, the flow comes into your brain, and four million other pieces of mechanism which you did not even know existed begin to operate.

The mind is the slayer of the soul. Even your bringing your mind to this process is murder. You have to draw the force inside, open, feel the flow of your life force. Until you can feel the flow of your life force circulating through you and flowing through you, what are you? You are filled with yourself. What are you? You are ego. Ego and insanity. You have to surrender *you*.

If you grow, what you are at this moment will not even exist in three months. Why analyze? Why try to understand something that will be dead six months from now?

Self-analysis is absolutely cracked, because it has no meaning. If you nourish something, it will not be that same something. If it grows, it will not be that same something. If you surrender it, it will not be that same something. So why spend the time being involved in one level of tension when you can grow and transcend it, and it will fall away from you like a dead skin in a very short period of time?

When you receive something it should come into you in a spiritual way and go through every muscle in your body. You should marinate in it: feel this thing flowing through and touching every organ, every muscle in your body, and going into your bones.

It is our mind that stops that, because the mind is the thing that breeds tension within us. We analyze. We try to understand. Inside our heart there should be a joyousness that wishes to receive that which is available for us as a human being. It is our blocks, our tensions, and all the things that have to do with the external human being that stop this flow and stop the feeling of this great joy and energy that exist in the atmosphere.

We always look for justification for our complexity instead of choosing simplicity, which has to do with surrendering and receiving.

———◆———

For me, having an ashram in California, in Texas, or any other place involves nothing more than the pleasure of going to see people whom I love very deeply and feel committed to. This is not work. The work I do has to do with breaking me down and surrendering me. The other is flow.

All one brings to the work is the opening through which the force can come. That force is the power. The human being, because of its physical nature, is nothing more than the restriction to this flow. You, when you sit and do your meditation, are a limitation to that which is trying to come through you.

———◆———

All I ever see in my growth, continually, is my limitation. I am grateful to see that, because I can never think so much of myself. The miracles that take place have to do with God. You give; it happens. You will be strong this way. You have to see your nothingness; only through that do you have the sense of Creation. It works not because of you; it works in spite of you. You can surrender and allow it. You can separate yourself from your own negativity, your own limitation, and give what you have been taught to give, and you will see a miracle take place.

————◆◆————

The impediments to the simplicity of our spiritual potential are, first, our lack of being open to the simplicity, and, second, our tension. All the things that respond, all the things that seem to know, are really the limitations. If you surrender them then the energy, the content of all this knowingness, goes deeper inside and opens a deeper part of you.

We have thousands and thousands of layers within ourselves. The energy from the top starts to break up and go into the next layer, and that breaks and goes into the next. It is a continual succession of enlightenment and surrender, so that the energy of the enlightenment soaks into the level below and frees you.

It is only by seeing our work and not being satisfied with it that we have the potential for growth. The tension builds up only when something in us feels secure and does not want to work again. We have inside us something that says "Ah, I've done this work for forty years." You feel sore, you feel tight, you feel tense. What you have succeeded in doing is exhausting a level of energy. But if you surrender, you go into a deeper level of dynamic, vital energy; and the energy to do the work exists in every level. You dig into a deeper level and you find everything exists within. It is fresh and real and exciting.

Rebirth

You have to die and have a rebirth here, on this earth, over and over again. Then, finally, you can open to your inner core.

You are not growing to justify what you are. Your whole purpose in working is to keep yourself open so that the energy can blend with you and you can have a death and a rebirth so you will *not* be what you are now. Because of the tremendous energy that you draw in, allow to flow within yourself, and use within yourself, you have a rebirth that goes on and on and on. That is the whole foundation of kundalini yoga.

This is why I do not care for people's general concepts of yoga. They are trying to embellish what is in them. But the point is to have it completely destroyed and to become a new being over and over again. It is rebirth that we are working for, not realization, because if you work for realization, what will be realized is what you are now. But if you die and you are reborn again and again, the person who has realization will be a much higher being than what you are now.

It is much better to invest yourself in rebirth than to invest yourself in realization. I certainly would not want me as I was twenty years ago to be realized. Who the hell wants that? To have someone who is ninety percent crazy and filled with tensions realized, what good can it be?

It is rebirth that we are working for. We want to have our rebirth many, many times. Then if we want realization at the end of our lives, fine — it will come with a much greater refinement, a much greater sense of consciousness inside.

You have to have rebirth. In other words, your whole system has to be refined. You have to die, shedding skin after skin after skin. You have to die and have a rebirth here, on this earth, over and over again. Then, finally, you can open to your inner core. But this spiritual development, this spiritual sensitivity, develops with rebirth, which means tremendous work and a tremendous sense of surrender so that God's will can be done.

The result is not what we think a spiritual person should be like. This expectation just breaks in you, and the next day you will see a million things that are different in yourself. It goes on again and again and again, and then you really can surrender. You come to your own true being that way.

———◆——

A rebirth is a very painful thing to go through, because it is the total detachment, at a particular time, from one dimension in favor of another. It takes more than a doctor to sit with you through that. It is like having every muscle in your body tear free. The pain is the only thing we are conscious of, because we do not understand that a rebirth is coming until the death is complete. Many people go through very difficult situations as they have their death. They sit with the death and cry about the death and moan and complain and pour all the rebirth energy into the death. The positive alternative that exists is minuscule compared to the huge drama of the death. Instead of looking for this little positive drop that allows for rebirth, and feeding it, they sit there complaining about all of the terrible things they have gone through, not understanding that those things have a purpose.

I have watched so many people destroy the energy within them at that particular stage. Life is perfect. Suffering is the essential drawing away of one energy to allow a new energy to come in. It is like losing people we love. Certainly we find it painful, but there is always a reward, another consciousness or sensitivity that is given. But we always moan about what we lose and we refuse to open and allow a new life to come in because we are afraid it will be taken away from us again. We should only be lucky enough to have our life taken away from us endlessly; we would become free. It takes this detachment, consciously, over and over and over again, to finally give us the maturity we need. It is like people who go through three bad marriages before they have the maturity for a good one. We have to give away and allow to be taken away from us this life that we have. It is not sufficient for the end purpose we are working toward. So we transcend and feel this death, feel the pain of it, while we reach for this new life. And if we do not have the concept of reaching for rebirth, then the pain will certainly have all been for nothing.

You have to try very deeply to understand this within the framework of your own life. Simultaneous with any situation that is ripping out of you is another situation that is opening for you. Only a lack of the concept of rebirth within our culture prevents this experience from being available for you.

———◆———

As we mature and grow spiritually we tend to be confused by the process of dying and being reborn. This is because we cannot separate levels within ourselves. We are caught in our mind, we are completely limited by past experience, by the way we were raised. We do not have the capacity to separate emotions, to separate ideas, to find within anything that which is good. If we see in a box of tomatoes one that is rotten, we will throw the whole box away. We discard so much of the depth of our life because of some superficial thing we see. With the whole process of growing based on a death, on one thing being destroyed to give life to something else, people endlessly complain and whine, and feel only that which is dying, instead of feeling that which is coming to life.

We have to become aware that to grow we have to be able to separate the growth process from the whole of our life. We have to see our objective there and to understand that these expressions have much less value and certainly have nothing to do with our attaining what we wish to attain. Going forward and paying a price is part of our reality; it is the only way we can expect to get to our objective. So as we work and we feel pain, we feel tensions, we feel confusion, we have to say, "Fine, what is the confusion?" We are going through a morass of stuff, we are going through a dusty hallway where we have so much of our garbage stored, not only from today, but from years past or lifetimes past. It has to be confusing. How could we make order out of a chaos that we have accumulated over thousands and thousands of years, or maybe even thousands of lifetimes?

We think when we work spiritually that we are in contact with reality. We are no more in contact with reality than a person in an insane asylum is in contact with reality. We are beginning to mix up levels. We are doing the one thing that is guaranteed to confuse us. We are trying to become more rational on our ordinary physical level, but at the same time we are reaching to another level. So we are doing two things simultaneously. We are trying to solidify one level and we are disturbing the level above it. This is the reason so much difficulty arises and so much confusion arises. You are reinforcing one thing and destroying another, like Shiva, who is the destroyer and the giver of life.

Only a fool can study spiritually and just feel lightness, joy, and sweetness. These should be there in spite of the level that is dying, in spite of that which is being destroyed. Your consciousness should become broad enough to encompass the lesser existence that is going away while you are relating to the higher existence that you are working toward. Unless you identify with this rebirth, it will never take place. All of your energy will go to the level of death and your energy will be absorbed in it. The energy will go into the descending instead of the transcending force. This is the time when transcending is essential.

I am trying to explain it to you so that when you encounter this type of event you will understand it. It does not mean you are not working well. It means you are working the best possible way that any human being can work.

———◆◆———

When the energy you are working with matures, and you begin to have a rebirth, you go through a kind of psychodrama. For the energy to go into a rebirth, your energy starts to go to a higher dimension. As you work and you start withdrawing on one dimension, your energy goes to another dimension. You begin to feel all kinds of strangeness in your chemistry. A lot of your physical energy is going to the level above this level and beginning to accumulate there as you are trying to build a new physical body and a new capacity in another dimension. So you feel a letting down or a detachment from your energy, which we always think of in a negative way.

We have a drop in energy because the energy we are working with is being used for two purposes at that point: to sustain the level on which we exist and also to prepare for this state of rebirth. So we are living on this level and being reborn on another level simultaneously. It takes a tremendous amount out of us. It is no different than a woman giving birth. We feel all kinds of strangeness.

One of the most extraordinary things about this whole event is that you are never conscious of a birth until after it takes place. So you are unaware of the reason for this change in your chemistry. Also, a void is usually created where the matter was that is leaving this level to go to the next level. A great deal of illusion is attracted to the area where this reality existed. So you begin to have hallucinations. You have all kinds of effects taking place around you. You feel a tremendous change of chemistry, all kinds of upsets, tensions, and burnings inside, things that make you anything but compatible with your fellow human beings. You are going through your ordinary physical, psychological, and spiritual life unaware of what is taking place.

You will find that your attention, instead of going into the realistic relationships and situations available for you, will try to go off into illusionary situations. It is as if you were in the cartoon business and you were making $100,000 a year making cartoons, and somebody came along and offered you a $2,000,000 movie. You get so involved in making this mythical $2,000,000 movie that you stop making your cartoons. Then the movie falls through, you are out of work, and you have to take a job as a waiter because you have destroyed your reality reaching for an illusion.

The only way to get a reality is to sustain the level of reality that you are on and allow the energy to grow there. It is very important that you consciously accept what is taking place at this particular stage.

When I am going through a rebirth, I know that I am dying, and I am very grateful for it. I sit quietly and I drink thirty-two cups of tea in my store. I try to read a murder mystery and stay as easy as I can, and very open, to allow myself to die. I do not want to feed energy into the death. This current reality is dying and on this level I feel terrible. I really feel terrible. But on the next floor there is something that is beginning to come to life.

I am conscious enough to allow that new life to come into being, even if I can't see it. I may see it the next day or a week from now. When I feel like this, even though I know there is no reason in the world for me to feel like this, because my life is wonderful, then I know a rational reason will not be found. The only possible reason is that something in me is trying to die. There is no sense trying to explain something that is not rational.

Working and transcending bring about a complete change of chemistry. People always want consistency, but there is nothing consistent about growing. The only thing consistent about it is that changes take place. You have to become aware of those changes. A simple way of seeing those changes is seeing them in nature. You can smell it. I can always tell when I am going through a big change. One clue is that I cannot drink coffee. Coffee tastes too bitter to me. That becomes a clue to me. My chemistry is not accepting this thing that it usually accepts; something is changing.

You have to look for clues. You have to look at the way you breathe: you are not breathing the same. You are breathing with the same effort, but you are not getting the same depth inside you. Why is that? Because something is changing over and you have to breathe differently — deeper, longer — to make this connection.

Your breathing is one of the great factors that can warn you about a change taking place in you. Other factors are your taste for food, your reaching out in a relationship, and what you require from somebody else. Usually, when you are rejecting somebody you ordinarily love, that is also an indication of a change taking place. You begin to reject people, you begin to reject situations that it is normal for you to be open to. That is also an expression of the change.

————◆————

In our ordinary spiritual work, we are trying to raise our energy to a higher dimension. We succeed in doing that by taking from this physical level. When we reach to the ultimate of the physical manifestation, or the height and refinement of the energy we are working with, it begins to break through into another dimension. Then we feel a tremendous drop in our vitality and simultaneously we attract these enormous illusionary situations. We do not have the capacity to support them. They become very much like the sirens in the *Odyssey* who appear on small islands and tempt the sailors passing in a ship to disembark. The boat going through the water is the symbol for the transition between one dimension and another. When you are in transition, that is not the time to stop off and investigate other strange and exotic worlds. By doing so you prolong your journey for an enormous time.

Almost everyone in a spiritual life makes so many side journeys. Sometimes people finish this physical life and never succeed in their own journey because they are so busy going here and there and seeing all these other things.

It is up to you to do the work you are capable of doing. Do it deeper and deeper and work with it more consciously, so you can finish this trip. And it is always when you reach the place where you are coming close to a new realization that all these other things appear to magnetize you. It has been amazing for me to see this. I sometimes can walk outside myself, and it is as if I open a door and there is a great fog outside, a great embankment of fog. I hear voices, and I see all kinds of apparitions walking around. They want me to come and start a relationship. But that is not the time to get involved in another relationship, it is the time to work inside, to take care of the simple reality that I am capable of handling.

I have not had a day in the last couple of weeks where I have not lost a $10,000 sale or a $3,000 sale, or a $5,000 sale. It is almost ridiculous; this type of thing becomes a drama that you see repeated until you can detach from it.

I have been very grateful to be detached from this phenomenon. It is completely separate from me; it has nothing to do with me. I am not putting my energy into having lost this or that big sale. I am grateful for my $200 sales and my $500 sales and whatever else it is that I have until I get through this period. I will live on short rations if I have to; I really do not care.

I am aware of the psychodrama that I am going through, and I am aware, more than anything else, of the purpose for which this is taking place. It is not a punishment. It is a temptation, a test to see if I will be stupid enough to get involved in illusions while I am going through a rebirth. I will not waste my energy paying attention to all of the external things that might happen. I am responsible for many, many small things that I can take care of. I go to sleep early, I try to wake up and talk to myself to make myself feel happier, and I accept what I have consciously and with gratitude.

It is chasing illusions that destroys the capacity for a reality. We understand that we are going through a transition by the appearance of temptations to do many things that sound extraordinary and that look very possible, and by our tendency to neglect the thing we are directly responsible for. So if you ever feel a drop in energy and all these other attractions coming simultaneously, then you must understand you are in a weakened condition and you cannot become exotic. It is not the time to be exotic, it is the time to be simple and be grateful that we do not succumb to illusions.

It is like going to a party where there are five hundred people, and running into Gina Lollobrigida. She comes over and says, "Big boy, I want you to take me away to the Islands for six weeks." Why do I have to go to the Islands with Gina Lollobrigida, and what does she need with me? It really is very much that kind of a situation. You have to look carefully and not be hit by the glamor and all these other things that, if you looked at them in the cold light of day, you really would not want. Your imagination wants it, but your need and your responsibility, all the things you are working for in the long run, have to count, not only for something, but they finally have to count for everything.

You have to, within yourself, try to understand the reality and the simplicity of the situation that exists for you, and take advantage of it. If you have to chase something that is not there, if you have to succumb to an illusion when you do not have the energy, then you are too stupid to do spiritual work,

and you are too stupid to have an ordinary life. We
have to feed our realities and starve our illusions. It
is essential in growing. If you grow up to a point and
begin to feel a strangeness, a dullness in your chemistry, a lack of desire to grow and to go to class, a re-
luctance to do the things you are responsible for in
your own commitment to yourself and your spiritual
life, you will know you are coming to a subtle point
in your own development. Then you must make a
conscious effort. You must go inside and cut through
this lethargy, this illusion, this tendency to run any-
where if somebody tells you some cock-and-bull story
about an experience they had in a strange, exotic, and
inaccessible place.

It is only a fool who cannot live simply, happi-
ly, and with gratitude. What is wanted is available.
The same goes for inside yourself. If you find you are
not growing fast enough, all you have to do is sit
down, take a deep breath in your heart, and ask deeper and deeper until you feel your heart being pene-
trated like you were pressing your finger into a layer
cake. You find you can open in a deeper way, you can
internalize your energy in a deeper way, and you really can reach for what your objective is by not wasting
your energy externally, but internalizing it in a way
that nourishes you.

It is only the energy that you consciously save
that you can bring through your chakras and up your
spinal column. This is energy that will fortify you, so
when you do reach this night of mystery and illusion,
you can just drink inside and begin to see the swirl
outside you as unreal and as lacking nourishment.

Then you can become consciously aware of your responsibility for the situations that are realistic and that exist for you. So you do not pursue things that are not in your interest, or within your capacity, at that time.

———◆———

When you raise your level of energy, you automatically have to change your mechanism. After you change your mechanism, you consciously have to reach for a deeper energy so that the mechanism can run in a deeper, more conscious way. So, spiritual work manifests when you increase your energy. Then you should wake up at night and feel that somebody is working on your insides. You feel wiring being changed, things touching your heart, something opening your brain. It is taking place in a spiritual dimension. I had thousands and thousands of operations like this. I used to wake up at night and hear "clink, clink, clink, clink," — little steel instruments hitting each other. This went on and on. I got sick and tired of smelling that formaldehyde and feeling bandages on my head and hearing the clink, clink of the instruments and having that light in my face. It made me sick to my stomach. But it went on.

This is real. It is not a fable. It is not an illusion. It is the reality of the changing nature of a human being. You are being changed because you have increased the level of your energy. So you submit consciously and as gracefully as you can to all of this garbage. "Clink, clink, clink," and you have more energy. Something from a higher level is outfitting you inside with the ability to take the next step.

You are responsible for having the vitality to attract these experiences and really feel them in depth. The only way you can attract them is by breathing in, holding your breath in, feeling an expansion take place, and feeling your life flow. As this life flow in you increases, it feeds the chakras. The chakras emit from inside them a necessary chemistry as they change. This chemistry in turn begins to change your mechanism. You do not have a spiritual life until you go through these changes and begin to see and hear them.

You do not become free by being afraid and stopping your work. You become free by being afraid and working and surrendering and transcending. Being afraid is a normal situation for someone who is starving, who is not taking in enough energy. You take in, you digest, you detach, and you can be afraid. You find you can go back, take, and detach, and take, and detach, and take. It is the symbol of death and rebirth. Whenever you detach, something dies. When you attach, you are reborn. This is very real. The act of going to sleep at night and waking up in the morning is to die and be reborn. Taking in energy is to die and be reborn.

We think exactly the opposite. We think that by holding on we have accomplished something. It is not true. Being afraid to detach is natural, because you do not know what living is about. Your inability to work consciously exists because you are afraid to grow and make a higher commitment. It is fear that keeps you from opening your heart and working, because if you really open your heart, you have to make a move, and it is easier to sit there and say you blew a fuse.

———◆———

Two thieves meet on Avenue A. One of them says to the other one, "What did you do this week? He answers, "I did $200. What did you do?" "I did $5,000." The other one asks, "Well, where?" He says, "I went up to 56th Street and Park Avenue."

If you stay in your own neighborhood, the pickings are pretty lousy because that area has been picked over. It is a poor neighborhood. Why should you keep opening in the same place? Move into a new neighborhood. Open and go out and out and out and out and out.

———◆———

Experiences are very subtle, and they certainly are mysterious, because they are taken in by the unconscious mind trying to open to something new.

We have to learn to keep our own counsel, to ask only the person we work under. So, when you have an experience, it is only normal that you be afraid. We accept within ourselves anything of an extraordinary nature, and we understand that when we ask within ourselves and we have the capacity to go inside and want to a tremendous degree, and keep wanting and asking until we feel something open in us, then we are preparing ourselves to meet an energy field.

This can show itself in many ways. It can come as an experience with the eyes open, it can come in a dream, it can come as a vision, or it can come as a thought. But this is a very sacred moment, and the energy within this has to be taken inside. We have to stay open to it and try consciously to nourish it by coming back to this place that is open and allowing more and more energy to flow. Once we have connected to something of a higher nature, it is essential to keep that connection open. The very nature of a higher psychic or creative experience is that it will come into being and will develop only when it is fed with the same material or vibration that brought about its conception. So we have to stay open; we have to keep the wish open in us while we feel this thing germinating and growing.

This can be a very difficult time for you, because you have a duality taking place. You have your ordinary life and you have a new birth, or a new type of creative energy, starting to function in you. And that is the test of any kind of creative gift: to see whether you have the capacity to sustain the vision, the idea, the experience, and not go crazy when your energy is being drawn here and there. You have to sustain two levels of existence simultaneously.

The only way to move from one dimension to another is to allow your energy to stay in this body and simultaneously send into this other dimension part of your ordinary energy. This is a sacrifice. It requires being conscious of what you want, just as a scientist working in a laboratory has to give night after night to pursuing an idea and working until he or she comes to some kind of an answer.

We have to learn to sustain what we want. Not to have visions and not to have wishes, but to have longevity. This is essential to bring anything of creation into the world. It takes nine months to bring a baby into the world, and it probably takes nine years to have a creative rebirth. It is stealing from your ordinary life part of the energy you have and bringing it to a deeper place in yourself. If you can't make a sacrifice for something deeper, then you will only be a dreamer who runs from thing to thing and never sees anything come to fruition. Gandhi spent years in jail working toward a goal. Every human being who was a leader of any kind gave years and years of his or her life. It really is to have an ideal that is within the capacity of a human being, and to pursue it, that is the test of a human being.

Spirituality is not about being where you think you should be. It is not about being where you want to be. Spirituality is about being on the highest point of an ascending energy that keeps growing and growing. As this energy grows, it completely destroys every level of truth as you live it. This does not mean the truth that has been destroyed was not real. It was real for the level on which you existed before.

With students, I am not interested in how long they are with me; I am just interested in one thing: whether or not they are strong enough to break up the horizontal level and continue growing. For myself, I do not want to limit myself by what I was. I do not think, "I did all this work to get to here." That is baloney. That is making a drama of your life and trying to build an image for yourself. The point is to keep growing. It is to have the courage to keep growing, even if it pulls apart the structure of your life. Then it is freeing you. There is nothing wrong with pulling apart the structure. What is wrong is to build yourself into a coffin and then stay there and try to justify it.

Either you are working to live on a higher level all the time and to have a rebirth all the time, or you are trying to find justification for staying the way you are. The whole point of what we do is to destroy matter, which is this horizontal plane we sit on: the earth. It is to translate this physical and material matter into spiritual force. This is our work.

———◆◆———

I am going to be forty-five years old in two weeks and I am still burning inside with the thirst to grow. I still have this wish, and it drives me crazy. And I can qualify, I can stand next to anyone, but who wants to measure oneself against anyone else? The only one to be measured by is God, and the only goal to work toward is to get there. It breaks my heart when I see people not wanting to grow, not reaching for that growth. Every day for me is a burning that I, in my heart and soul, would never wish to inflict on anyone else. For me to serve you, I have to completely destroy within myself today, everything that existed for me yesterday, and tomorrow, everything from today. That way I do not crystallize, I do not become secure within myself and think I have gone far enough to qualify for what somebody else calls enlightenment. I do not want that. I want to die open. I want to go up. All the intelligence, all the crystallization, all the intellectualism can stay here and be eaten by those people who want to eat, like jackals, the truth of yesterday. It is only a dead truth.

Real truth is the continual destruction within yourself of everything that existed one moment before. If you have a need in yourself to hold onto anything, you will not only not have realization, but you will also not have within yourself the ability to be of service to other people. You will be a person who is offering death to other people because you do not have the capacity to go through the cycle of rebirth and death continually in yourself.

Either you want to grow in such a depth that you feel the cycle of death and rebirth in you at all times, or you do not really qualify to do this work. I would rather have people leave early on than to have them sit here and become a limitation for anyone else or a limitation for me. We have undoubtedly the most difficult spiritual work that is available. You have to make up your mind whether you really wish to grow, whether you really wish to surrender *you*, or you wish to hold on to six million extraneous things that have not nourished anybody for the past ten thousand years.

It is not the past that is needed, it is the moment that is needed. You need the capacity to assimilate the energy as it comes into the universe fresh. It has to go into you and root out everything that existed in you, not only in this life but in every past life. The only thing I promise you in return is an extraordinary life, a very remarkable life. You will see in yourself and in the connection that you have with other people a very living and creative experience. It is a dedication within yourself to reach toward this endlessness that has to do with our creative capacity. We have to be like any other organic entity. We have to live fresh every day and not try in any way to live in the past. We have to open and allow this energy to come into us and to burn out whatever was.

We see the smoke rising from the compost heap of our life as we take in this energy and loosen up deep within ourselves, in this unconsciousness that is so strongly embedded within us. We free ourselves and find that we can breathe. We find that these chakras that we have are not limited to our physical body, but they reach out into infinity. We can draw from thousands and thousands of years ago and millions of miles away the energy that we need. Spirituality, or cosmic consciousness, should not be so many words; it should be a living reality we can come to every single day within ourselves. We can see our world expand, we can feel every muscle within us open. The spiritual force becomes a nourishment that frees us. It frees our heart, it frees our eyes, it frees our mind, it frees every chakra within us so that we are not the slave of these organs, but we are free to feed them and have them expand and have them flow one to the other and bring us the nourishment that allows us to get above the earth.

Index

Realization, 169-70
Religion, 140-1
Relationships, 145-6
Renunciation, 149
Resistance, 65, 114, 124-8
Responsibility, 32, 37, 39, 40,
  45-6, 139, 141, 142;
  in class, 82
Root system, 136, 137, 140-1
Rudi, 3-4, 5, 6-15;
  in India, 26;
  first yoga teacher of, 57
Rudra, 4

Sacrifice, 149-50, 186
Self-acceptance, 138
Self-hatred, 136
Self-satisfaction, 164
Service, 27, 30, 92;
  to God, 41
Sexual attachment, 146
Sexual energy, 148
Sexuality, 148-9
Shankaracharya of Puri, 3,
  112
Shiva, 4, 173
Siddhartha, 50
Simplicity, 9, 25-6, 104-5,
  106, 163
Sleep, 142, 179
Spine, rotating the, 73, 76
Spiritual attainments, 119
Spiritual exercise. *See*
  Double-breath exercise.
Spirituality, 32, 33, 38, 39,
  46, 189
Spiritual knowledge, 59
Spiritual life, 27, 39-40
Spiritual materialism, 8

Spiritual practice, 11, 71-97
Spiritual work, 35-51;
  versus meditation, 40-42
Spiritual world, 39
Structure, 60, 187
Student, 55, 56, 62-3, 68, 187
  See also Teacher and
  student relationship.
Superiority, 41, 42
Surrender, 10, 41-2, 65, 95-6,
  108, 150, 153-65, 170
Sweetness, 38

Talking, 26, 38
Teacher, 3, 4, 56, 62, 64, 65,
  66-8;
  drawing from, 58-60;
  opening to, 58-61, 66-7
Teacher and student
  relationship, 4-6, 53-69,
  126
Teaching, 5, 59, 61
Temptation, 179-180
Tension, 8, 11-12, 20, 21, 25,
  29, 76, 94, 99-115, 138,
  162, 164
Test, 92, 179
Time and space, 13
Transcending, 86, 89-90,
  122, 140
Tree of Life, 140-1
Truth, 188

Unconsciousness, 105, 121

Vietnam war, 31
Visions, 77-8
Vow, 144

Wheel of fate, 113
Will, 120
Wish to grow, 28, 117-131
Words, 59
Work, 8, 10, 38, 115, 128, 160,
    174-5
Worthiness, 27-8

Yoga, 85, 169